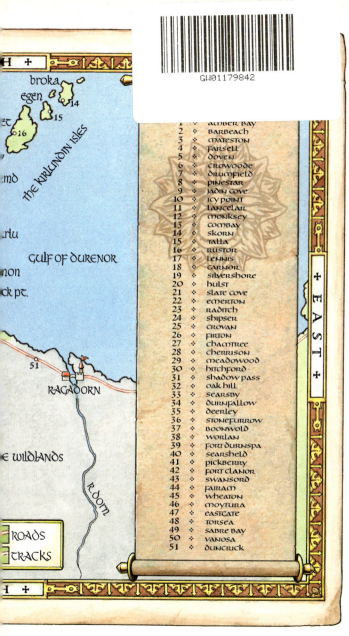

broka
egen
14
15
16

THE KIRLUNDIN ISLES

GULF OF DURENOR

ck pt.

51

RAGADORN

E WILDLANDS

R. DORN

ROADS

TRACKS

H + E A S T +

 he bearer of
this scroll,

name _____

is a _____

in the Order of the Kai

LONE WOLF 19
WOLF'S BANE

THE AUTHOR

JOE DEVER was born in 1956 at Woodford Bridge in Essex. After he left college, he became a professional musician, working in studios in Europe and America. While working in Los Angeles in 1977, he discovered a game called 'Dungeons and Dragons' and was soon an enthusiastic player. Five years later he won the Advanced Dungeons and Dragons Championships in the US, where he was the only British competitor. The award-winning Lone Wolf adventures are the culmination of many years of developing the world of Magnamund. They are printed in several languages and sold throughout the world.

LONE WOLF CLUB

The Lone Wolf Club offers its members regular newsletters which are packed with information about the *Lone Wolf* series. There are prize competitions, *Lone Wolf* stories, and regular special offers. Members also get the chance to collect *Lone Wolf* books signed by Joe Dever. If you are interested in membership details, please send an SAE to: The Lone Wolf Club, 39 Corfe Way, Broadstone, Dorset BH18 9ND, UK. If you live outside the UK (including Eire) please include two international reply coupons (IRCs).

LONE WOLF

Joe Dever

Illustrated by Brian Williams
Cover by Peter Jones

RED FOX

A Red Fox Book
Published by Random House Children's Books
A division of Random House UK Ltd
20 Vauxhall Bridge Road, London SW1V 2SA
London Melbourne Sydney Auckland
Johannesburg and agencies throughout the world

First published by Red Fox 1993
Text © Joe Dever 1993
Illustrations © Brian Williams 1993

Set in Souvenir Light
by Intype, London

Printed and bound in Great Britain
by Cox & Wyman Ltd, Reading

ISBN 0-09-998440 7

For Caroline Thomas, Margaret Conroy & Sue Mongredien

GRAND MASTER DISCIPLINES   NOTES

1	
2	
3	
4	
5*	
6*	
7*	
8*	
9*	
10*	

BACKPACK (max. 10 articles)	MEALS
1	
2	
3	
4	
5	−3 EP if no Meal available when instructed to eat.
6	BELT POUCH Containing Gold Crowns (50 maximum)
7	
8	
9	
10	

CS = COMBAT SKILL   EP = ENDURANCE POINTS

* 1 extra Discipline for every Grand Master adventure you have already completed.

ACTION CHART

COMBAT SKILL	ENDURANCE POINTS
	0 = dead

COMBAT RECORD

ENDURANCE POINTS   **ENDURANCE POINTS**

LONE WOLF	COMBAT RATIO	ENEMY
LONE WOLF	COMBAT RATIO	ENEMY
LONE WOLF	COMBAT RATIO	ENEMY
LONE WOLF	COMBAT RATIO	ENEMY
LONE WOLF	COMBAT RATIO	ENEMY

GRAND MASTER RANK

SPECIAL ITEMS LIST

DESCRIPTION	KNOWN EFFECTS

WEAPONS LIST

WEAPONS (maximum 2 Weapons)
1
2
If Holding Weapon and appropriate Grand Weaponmastery in combat +5 CS

GRAND WEAPONMASTERY CHECKLIST

DAGGER		SPEAR	
MACE		SHORT SWORD	
WARHAMMER		BOW	
AXE		SWORD	
QUARTERSTAFF		BROADSWORD	

QUIVER AND ARROWS

Quiver	No. of arrows carried
YES/NO	

THE STORY SO FAR . . .

You are Grand Master Lone Wolf, the sole survivor of a massacre that wiped out the First Order of the Kai – the warrior elite of Sommerlund.

It is the year MS 5080, thirty years since your brave kinsmen perished at the hands of the Darklords of Helgedad. These champions of evil, who were sent forth by Naar – the King of the Darkness – to destroy the fertile world of Magnamund have themselves since been destroyed. You vowed to avenge the murder of the Kai and you kept your pledge, for it was you who brought about their downfall when alone you infiltrated their foul domain – the Darklands – and caused the destruction of their leader and the base of his power that was the infernal city of Helgedad.

In the wake of their destruction, chaos befell the Darkland armies that had been poised to conquer all of Magnamund. Their disorder escalated into a mutinous civil war which allowed the freestate armies of Magnamund time in which to recover and launch a successful counter-offensive. Against the odds, a swift and total victory was secured over the feuding Darklands armies.

For ten unbroken years peace has reigned in Sommerlund. Under your direction the once-ruined monastery of the Kai has been rebuilt and restored to its former glory, and the task of teaching a New Order of Kai warriors the skills and proud traditions of your ancestors is also well established. The new generation of Kai recruits, all of whom were born during the era of war against the Darklords, possess strong latent Kai skills and all show exceptional promise. These skills will be nurtured and honed to perfection during their time at the monastery so that they may teach and inspire future generations, thereby ensuring the continued security of your homeland in future years.

Your attainment of the rank of Kai Grand Master brought with it great rewards. Some, such as the restoration of the Kai and the undying gratitude of your fellow Sommlending, could have been anticipated. Yet there have also been rewards which you could not possibly have foreseen. The discovery that within you lay the potential to develop Kai Disciplines beyond those of the Magnakai (which were thought to be the ultimate that a Kai Master could aspire to) was truly a revelation. Your discovery has inspired you to search for the wisdom and power that no Kai lord before you has ever possessed. In the name of your creator, the God Kai, and for the greater glory of Sommerlund and the Goddess Ishir, you have vowed to reach the very pinnacle of Kai perfection – to attain all of the Grand Master Disciplines and become the first Kai Supreme Master.

With diligence and determination you set about the restoration of the Kai Monastery and the training of the New Order recruits. Your efforts were soon rewarded for within the space of two short years, the first raw recruits had graduated to become a cadre of gifted Kai Masters who, in turn, were able to commence the teaching of their skills to subsequent intakes of Kai novices. The Kai Masters rose readily to their new-found responsibilities, leaving you free to devote more of your time to the pursuit and perfection of the Grand Master Disciplines. During this period you also received expert tutelage in the ways of magic from two of your most trusted friends and advisors: Guildmaster Banedon, leader of the Brotherhood of the Crystal Star, and Lord Rimoah, speaker for the High Council of the Elder Magi.

In the deepest subterranean level of the monastery, one hundred feet below the Tower of the Sun, you ordered the excavation and construction of a special vault. In this magnificent chamber wrought of granite and gold, you placed the seven Lorestones of Nyxator – gems of Kai power which you had recovered during an earlier quest for Kai knowledge. In this vault, bathed in the golden light of the radiant gems, you spent countless hours in pursuit of perfection. Sometimes alone, sometimes in the company of your two able advisors – Banedon and Rimoah – you worked hard to develop your innate Grand Master Disciplines, and grasp the fundamental secrets of Brotherhood and Old Kingdom magic. During this time you noticed many remarkable changes taking place within your body; you became physically and mentally stronger, your five primary senses sharpened far beyond all that you had experienced before, and, perhaps most remarkably, your body began to age at a much slower rate. Now, for every five years that elapse you age but one year.

In the years since your victory over the Darklords, peace has reigned victorious and the peoples of the Free Kingdoms have rejoiced in the knowledge that the evil which once threatened to destroy them has been banished from the face of Magnamund. Men have readily exchanged their swords for hoes and their shields for ploughs, and now the only marching they do is along the ruts of their freshly furrowed fields. Few are the watchful eyes that scan the distant horizon in fear of what may appear, although there are still some who maintain their vigilance, for the agents of the Dark God Naar come in many guises and there are those upon Magnamund who wait quietly in the shadows for the chance to do his evil bidding.

Already your new-found skills have been tested against Naar's agents and you have, on each occasion, acquitted yourself admirably. Yet your continuing victories have enraged the Dark God and inflamed his lust for vengeance. Three years earlier, you and your new Kai kinsmen achieved a glorious victory over a host of deadly Lavas. These dragon-like horrors were sent by Naar to destroy the Kai Monastery and lay waste to Sommerlund, and yet, despite their supernatural strength, they were defeated in battle by the sheer courage and skill of the New Order Kai who fought magnificently under your leadership.

After the ignominious defeat of his minions, Naar retreated to the Plane of Darkness to plot and scheme anew. Victory at the monastery had won for you a respite in the Dark God's war against Sommerlund and the Kai. The following three years were peaceful for your homeland, yet elsewhere on Magnamund the agents of Naar continued their insidious work. On several occasions your special skills were sought by envoys from foreign realms whose leaders were desperate to rid themselves of Naar's minions. Courageously you undertook many of these dangerous missions and, by succeeding where no other mortal could, you brought fresh glories upon yourself and your fellow Kai.

In the summer of MS 5080, during a return voyage by sea from a successful quest to distant Dessi, an act of sabotage very nearly wrecked the sailing ship that was transporting you home. Only fair weather and skilful repairs by the Sommlending crew saved the ship from being lost in the Gulf of Durenor. When the damaged craft limped into its home port of Anskaven, more than two weeks late, the reception you received was far from welcoming. The normally cheerful seafaring folk of this busy port were in a strangely sullen mood. Clearly they all recognized you, yet none cheered as you disembarked on Anskaven quay. The crowd were quietly hostile. Before you could determine their reasons, the uneasy silence was shattered by a troop of heavily-armoured cavalrymen who came galloping along the quayside, their gleaming swords drawn. The crowd scattered as the horsemen drew up in a circle around you. Their leader, a nervous young lieutenant whose coat bore the black eagle and three hearts motif of Avan Caldar, Baron of Anskaven, curtly ordered you to lay down your weapons. Not wishing to provoke these city troopers, you obeyed the command and allowed them to escort you to Baron Caldar's castle where you felt sure their inglorious mistake would be swiftly punished.

Baron Caldar formally received you in the Great

Hall of his castle. You had met previously on many state occasions at King Ulnar's court in Holmgard and had always held each other in high esteem. Yet Caldar, flanked by more than a dozen armed bodyguards, could barely bring himself to conceal his contempt. He spoke to you as if you were a hated criminal. You asked why you were being treated in such a manner, but your pleas fell on deaf ears. Without further explanation, he ordered that you be taken immediately to the dungeons and placed in irons.

Later that evening, using your mental Kai Disciplines to help loosen the tight-lipped resolve of a dungeon guard, you learned the reasons for your apparent fall from grace.

'You first arrived in Anskaven by ship eighteen days ago, as expected,' said the gaoler, in response to your psychic commands. 'Baron Caldar met you personally at the quayside and gave you a horse and six of his best troopers to escort you to Toran. During your ride to that city, they say you murdered his men and burnt their bodies. On arriving at Toran, you tried to assassinate Banedon – the Guildmaster of the Brotherhood of the Crystal Star. He survived, yet much of the Guildmaster's Hall was destroyed by your doing. To cover your escape from the city, you poisoned the wells causing hundreds of deaths. At first it was said that a Helghast had adopted your likeness to gain entry to the Guildhall, but Guildmaster Banedon refuted these claims. He is convinced that you are possessed by the spirit of Naar. The Guildmaster dispatched the Toran militia to spread this message across Sommerlund. A few days later at the forest village of Durnfallow, near Tyso, the Fryearl of Durnfallow was murdered and his manor house was torched to the ground. The villagers say they saw you riding away from the blazing ruins, howling like a crazed wolf. The people are terrified by the thought that Naar has corrupted you – their greatest hero – and turned you against your own. They are scared and they are demanding swift justice. King Ulnar has bowed to their will; he has sent all of his Border Rangers to Tyso with orders to find and kill you on sight.'

The news of your alleged crimes comes as a bitter blow. You are sure that it is all the handiwork of an agent of Naar, and you resolve to find and vanquish this impostor at the first opportunity. However, as you cast your eyes around the damp walls of the castle dungeon, you can only pray to Ishir and Kai that the Baron and his guards will believe your story and allow you a chance to reclaim your honour.

THE GAME RULES

You keep a record of your adventure on the *Action Chart* that you will find in the front of this book. For ease of use, and for further adventuring, it is recommended that you photocopy these pages.

For more than ten years, ever since the demise of the Darklords of Helgedad, you have devoted yourself to developing further your fighting prowess – COMBAT SKILL – and physical stamina – ENDURANCE. Before you begin this Grand Master adven-

17

ture you need to measure how effective your training has been. To do this take a pencil and, with your eyes closed, point the blunt end of it on to the *Random Number Table* on the last page of the book. If you pick a 0 it counts as zero.

The first number that you pick from the *Random Number Table* in this way represents your COMBAT SKILL. Add 25 to the number you picked and write the total in the COMBAT SKILL section of your *Action Chart* (ie, if your pencil fell on the number 6 in the *Random Number Table* you would write in a COMBAT SKILL of 31). When you fight, your COMBAT SKILL will be pitted against that of your enemy. A high score in this section is therefore very desirable.

The second number that you pick from the *Random Number Table* represents your powers of ENDURANCE. Add 30 to this number and write the total in the ENDURANCE section of your *Action Chart* (ie, if your pencil fell on the number 7 on the *Random Number Table* you would have 37 ENDUR-ANCE points).

If you are wounded in combat you will lose ENDUR-ANCE points. If at any time your ENDURANCE points fall to zero, you are dead and the adventure is over. Lost ENDURANCE points can be regained during the course of the adventure, but your number of ENDURANCE points can not rise above the number you have when you start an adventure.

Playing Tip: You may use a 10-sided die instead of the *Random Number Table* if you find it easier.

If you have successfully completed any of the previous adventures in the *Lone Wolf* series

(Books 1–18), you can carry your current scores of COMBAT SKILL and ENDURANCE points over to Book 19. These scores may include Weaponmastery, Curing, and Psi-surge bonuses obtained upon completion of *Lone Wolf Kai* (Books 1–5) or *Magnakai* (Books 6–12) adventures. Only if you have completed these previous adventures will you benefit from the appropriate bonuses in the course of the Grand Master series. You may also carry over any Weapons and Backpack Items you had in your possession at the end of your last adventure, and these should be entered on your new Grand Master *Action Chart* (you are still limited to two Weapons, but you may now carry up to ten Backpack Items). However, only the following Special Items may be carried over from the *Lone Wolf Kai* (Books 1–5) and *Magnakai* (Books 6–12) series to the *Lone Wolf Grand Master* series (Books 13 onwards):

Crystal star pendant	Jewelled mace
Sommerswerd	Silver bow of Duadon
Silver helm	Silver bracers
Kagonite chainmail	Korlinium scabbard

KAI & MAGNAKAI DISCIPLINES

During your distinguished rise to the rank of Kai Grand Master you have become proficient in all of the basic Kai and Magnakai Disciplines. These Disciplines have provided you with a formidable arsenal of natural abilities which have served you well in the fight against the agents and champions of Naar, King of the Darkness. A brief summary of your skills is given below:

Weaponmastery
Proficiency with all close combat and missile weapons. Master of unarmed combat; no COMBAT SKILL loss when fighting bare-handed.

Animal Control
Communication with most animals; limited control over hostile creatures. Can use woodland animals as guides and can block a non-sentient creature's sense of taste and smell.

Curing
Steady restoration of lost ENDURANCE points (to self and others) as a result of combat wounds. Neutralization of poisons, venoms & toxins. Repair of serious battle wounds.

Invisibility
Mask body heat and scent; hide effectively; mask sounds during movement; minor alterations of physical appearance.

Huntmastery
Effective hunting of food in the wild; increased agility; intensified vision, hearing, smell and night vision.

Pathsmanship
Read languages, decipher symbols, read footprints & tracks. Intuitive knowledge of compass points;

detection of enemy ambush up to 500 yds; ability to cross terrain without leaving tracks; converse with sentient creatures; mask self from psychic spells of detection.

Psi-surge
Attack enemies using the powers of the mind; set up disruptive vibrations in objects; confuse enemies.

Psi-screen
Defence against – hypnosis, supernatural illusions, charms, hostile telepathy, and evil spirits. Ability to divert and re-channel hostile psychic energy.

Nexus
Move small items by projection of mind power; withstand extremes of temperature; extinguish fire by force of will; limited immunity to flames, toxic gases, corrosive liquids.

Divination
Sense imminent danger; detect invisible or hidden enemy; telepathic communication; recognize magic-using and/or magical creatures; detect psychic residues; limited ability to leave body and spirit-walk.

GRAND MASTER DISCIPLINES

Now, through the pursuit of new skills and the further development of your innate Kai abilities, you have set out upon a path of discovery that no other Kai Grand Master has ever attempted with success. Your determination to become the first Kai Supreme Master, by acquiring total proficiency in all twelve of the Grand Master Disciplines, is an awe-inspiring challenge. You will be venturing into the unknown, pushing back the boundaries of human limitation in the pursuit of greatness and the cause of Good. May the blessings of the gods Kai and Ishir go with you on your brave and noble quest.

In the years following the demise of the Darklords you have reached the rank of Kai Grand Defender, which means that you have mastered *four* of the Grand Master Disciplines listed below. It is up to you to choose which four Disciplines these are. As all of the Grand Master Disciplines will be of use to you at some point during your adventure, pick your four skills with care. The correct use of a Grand Master Discipline at the right time could save your life. When you have chosen your four Disciplines, enter them in the Grand Master Disciplines section of your *Action Chart*.

Grand Weaponmastery
This Discipline enables a Grand Master to become supremely efficient in the use of all weapons. When you enter combat with one of your Grand Master weapons, you add 5 points to your COMBAT SKILL. The rank of Kai Grand Defender, with which you begin the Grand Master series, means you are skilled in *two* of the weapons listed opposite and overleaf.

Animal Mastery
Grand Masters have considerable control over hostile, non-sentient creatures. Also, they have the ability to converse with birds and fishes, and use them as guides.

Deliverance (*Advanced Curing*)
Grand Masters are able to use their healing power to repair serious battle wounds. If, whilst in combat, their COMBAT SKILL is reduced to 8 points or less, they can draw upon their mastery to restore 20 ENDURANCE points. This ability can only be used once every 20 days.

Assimilance (*Advanced Invisibility*)
Grand Masters are able to effect striking changes to their physical appearance, and maintain these changes over a period of a few days. They have also mastered advanced camouflage techniques that make them virtually undetectable in an open landscape.

Grand Huntmastery
Grand Masters are able to see in total darkness, and have greatly heightened senses of touch and taste.

Grand Pathsmanship
Grand Masters are able to resist entrapment by hostile plants, and have a super-awareness of ambush, or the threat of ambush, in woods and dense forests.

Kai-surge

When using their psychic ability to attack an enemy, Grand Masters may add 8 points to their COMBAT SKILL. For every round in which Kai-surge is used, they need only deduct 1 ENDURANCE point. Grand Masters have the option of using a weaker form of psychic attack called **Mindblast**. When using this lesser attack, they may add 4 points to their COMBAT SKILL without loss of ENDURANCE points. (Kai-surge, Psi-surge, and Mindblast cannot be used simultaneously.)

Grand Masters cannot use Kai-surge if their ENDURANCE score falls to 6 points or below.

Kai-screen

In psychic combat, Grand Masters are able to construct mind fortresses capable of protecting themselves and others. The strength and capacity of these fortresses increases as a Grand Master advances in rank.

Grand Nexus

Grand Masters are able to withstand contact with harmful elements, such as flames and acids, for upwards of an hour in duration. This ability increases as a Grand Master advances in rank.

Telegnosis (*Advanced Divination*)

This Discipline enables a Grand Master to spirit-walk for far greater lengths of time, and with far fewer ill effects. Duration, and the protection of his inanimate body, increases as a Grand Master advances in rank.

Magi-Magic

Under the tutelage of Lord Rimoah, you have been able to master the rudimentary skills of battle magic, as taught to the Vakeros – the native warriors of Dessi. These skills include the use of basic magi-magic spells such as *Shield*, *Power Word*, and *Invisible Fist*. As you advance in rank, so will your knowledge and mastery of Old Kingdom magic increase.

Kai-alchemy

Under the tutelage of Guildmaster Banedon, you have mastered the elementary spells of Left-handed magic, as practised by the Brotherhood of the Crystal Star. These spells include *Lightning Hand*, *Levitation*, and *Mind Charm*. As you advance in rank, so will your knowledge and mastery of Left-handed magic increase, enabling you eventually to craft new Kai weapons and artifacts.

If you successfully complete the mission as set in Book 19 of the *Lone Wolf Grand Master* series, you may add a further Grand Master Discipline of your choice to your *Action Chart* in Book 20. For every Grand Master Discipline you possess, in excess of the original four Disciplines you begin with, you may add 1 point to your basic COMBAT SKILL score and 2 points to your basic ENDURANCE points score. These bonus points, together with your extra Grand Master Discipline(s), your original four Grand Master Disciplines, and any Special Items that you have found and been able to keep during your adventures, may then be carried over and used in the next Grand Master adventure, which is called: *The Curse of Naar*.

EQUIPMENT

Before you set off on your long journey home to Sommerlund, you took with you a map of Northern Magnamund (see the inside front cover of this book) and a pouch of gold. To find out how much gold is in the pouch, pick a number from the *Random Number Table* and add 20 to the number you have picked. The total equals the number of Gold Crowns inside the pouch, and you should now enter this number in the 'Gold Crowns' section of your *Action Chart*.

If you have successfully completed any of the previous *Lone Wolf* adventures (Books 1–18), you may add this sum to the total sum of Crowns you already possess. Fifty Crowns is the maximum you can carry, but additional Crowns can be left in safe-keeping at your monastery.

You can take four items from the list below, again adding to these, if necessary, any you may already possess from previous adventures (remember, you are still limited to two Weapons, but you may now carry a maximum of ten Backpack Items).

BROADSWORD (Weapons)

BOW (Weapons)

QUIVER (Special Items) This contains six arrows; record them on your Weapons List.

DAGGER (Weapons)

SWORD (Weapons)

2 MEALS (Meals) Each Meal takes up one space in your Backpack.

ROPE (Backpack Item)

POTION OF LAUMSPUR (Backpack Item) This potion restores 4 ENDURANCE points to your total when swallowed after combat. There is enough for only one dose.

AXE (Weapons)

List the four items that you choose on your *Action Chart*, under the appropriate headings, and make a note of any effect that may have on your ENDURANCE points or COMBAT SKILL.

Equipment – How to use it

Weapons
The maximum number of weapons that you can carry is *two*. Weapons aid you in combat. If you have the Grand Master Discipline of Grand Weaponmastery and a correct weapon, it adds 5 points to your COMBAT SKILL. If you find a weapon during your adventure, you may pick it up and use it.

Bows and Arrows
During your adventure there will be opportunities to use a bow and arrow. If you equip yourself with this weapon, and you possess at least one arrow, you may use it when the text of a particular section allows you to do so. The bow is a useful weapon,

28

for it enables you to hit an enemy at a distance. However, a bow cannot be used in hand-to-hand combat, therefore it is recommended that you also equip yourself with a close combat weapon, such as a sword or an axe.

In order to use a bow you must possess a quiver and at least one arrow. Each time the bow is used, erase an arrow from your *Action Chart*. A bow cannot, of course, be used if you exhaust your supply of arrows, but the opportunity may arise during your adventure for you to replenish your stock of arrows.

If you have the Discipline of Grand Weaponmastery with a bow, you may add 3 points to any number you choose from the *Random Number Table*, when using the bow.

Backpack Items
These must be stored in your Backpack. Because space is limited, you may keep a maximum of ten articles, including Meals, in your Backpack at any one time. You may only carry one Backpack at a time. During your travels you will discover various useful items which you may decide to keep. You may exchange or discard them at any point when you are not involved in combat.

Any item that may be of use, and which can be picked up on your adventure and entered on your *Action Chart* is given either initial capitals (eg Gold Dagger, Magic Pendant), or is clearly identified as a Backpack Item. Unless you are told that it is a Special Item, carry it in your Backpack.

Special Items

Special Items are not carried in the Backpack. When you discover a Special Item, you will be told how or where to carry it. The maximum number of Special Items that can be carried on any adventure is twelve.

Food

Food is carried in your Backpack. Each Meal counts as one item. You will need to eat regularly during your adventure. If you do not have any food when you are instructed to eat a Meal, you will lose 3 ENDURANCE points. However, if you have chosen the Discipline of Grand Huntmastery, you will not need to tick off a Meal when instructed to eat.

Potion of Laumspur

This is a healing potion that can restore 4 ENDURANCE points to your total when swallowed after combat. There is enough for one dose only. If you discover any other potion during the adventure, you will be informed of its effect. All potions are Backpack Items.

RULES FOR COMBAT

There will be occasions during your adventure when you will have to fight an enemy. The enemy's COMBAT SKILL and ENDURANCE points are given in the text. Lone Wolf's aim in the combat is to kill the enemy by reducing his ENDURANCE points to zero while losing as few ENDURANCE points as possible himself.

At the start of a combat, enter Lone Wolf's and the enemy's ENDURANCE points in the appropriate boxes on the *Combat Record* section of your *Action Chart*.

The sequence for combat is as follows:

1. Add any extra points gained through your Grand Master Disciplines and Special Items to your current COMBAT SKILL total.
2. Subtract the COMBAT SKILL of your enemy from this total. The result is your **Combat Ratio**. Enter it on the *Action Chart*.

   Example
   Lone Wolf (COMBAT SKILL 32) is attacked by a pack of Doomwolves (COMBAT SKILL 30). He is taken by surprise and is not given the opportunity of evading their attack. Lone Wolf has the Grand Master Discipline of Kai-surge to which the Doomwolves are not immune, so Lone Wolf adds 8 points to his COMBAT SKILL giving him a total COMBAT SKILL of 40.

   He subtracts the Doomwolf pack's COMBAT SKILL from his own, giving a *Combat Ratio* of +10 (40-30=+10). +10 is noted on the *Action Chart* as the *Combat Ratio*.

3. When you have your *Combat Ratio*, pick a number from the *Random Number Table*.
4. Turn to the Combat Results Table on the inside back cover of this book. Along the top of the chart are shown the *Combat Ratio* numbers.

Find the number that is the same as your *Combat Ratio* and cross-reference it with the random number that you have picked (the random numbers appear on the side of the chart). You now have the number of ENDURANCE points lost by both Lone Wolf and his enemy in this round of combat. (*E* represents points lost by the enemy; *LW* represents points lost by Lone Wolf.)

Example

The *Combat Ratio* between Lone Wolf and the Doomwolf Pack has been established as +10. If the number taken from the *Random Number Table* is a 2, then the result of the first round of combat is:

Lone Wolf loses 3 ENDURANCE points (plus an additional 1 point for using Kai-surge. This loss is in addition to the loss suffered as a result of combat.)

Doomwolf Pack loses 9 ENDURANCE points.

5. On the *Action Chart*, mark the changes in ENDURANCE points to the participants in the combat.
6. Unless otherwise instructed, or unless you have an option to evade, the next round of combat now starts.
7. Repeat the sequence from Stage 3.

This process of combat continues until ENDURANCE points of either the enemy or Lone Wolf are reduced to zero, at which point the one with the zero score is declared dead. If Lone Wolf is dead, the adventure is over. If the enemy is dead, Lone

Wolf proceeds but with his ENDURANCE points reduced.

A summary of Combat Rules appears on the page after the *Random Number Table*.

Evasion of combat

During your adventure you may be given the chance to evade combat. If you have already engaged in a round of combat and decide to evade, calculate the combat for that round in the usual manner. All points lost by the enemy as a result of that round are ignored, and you make your escape. Only Lone Wolf may lose ENDURANCE points during that round (but then that is the risk of running away!) You may only evade if the text of the particular section allows you to do so.

LEVELS OF KAI GRAND MASTERSHIP

The following table is a guide to the rank and titles you can achieve at each stage of your journey along the road of Kai Grand Mastership. As you complete each adventure successfully in the *Lone Wolf Grand Master* series, you will gain an additional Grand Master Discipline and progress towards the pinnacle of Kai perfection – to become a Kai Supreme Master.

No. of Grand Master Disciplines acquired	Grand Master Rank
1	Kai Grand Master Senior
2	Kai Grand Master Superior
3	Kai Grand Sentinel
4	Kai Grand Defender – *You begin the Lone Wolf Grand Master adventures at this level of mastery*
5	Kai Grand Guardian
6	Sun Knight
7	Sun Lord
8	Sun Thane
9	Grand Thane
10	Grand Crown
11	Sun Prince
12	Kai Supreme Master

IMPROVED GRAND MASTER
DISCIPLINES

As you rise through the higher levels of Kai Grand Mastery you will find that your Disciplines will steadily improve. For example, if you possess the Discipline of Grand Nexus when you reach the Grand Master rank of Grand Thane, you will be able to pass freely through Shadow Gates and explore the nether realms of Aon and the Daziarn Plane.

If you are a Grand Master who has reached the rank of Grand Crown, you will now benefit from improvements to the following Grand Master Disciplines:

Grand Weaponmastery
Kai Grand Crowns with this discipline are consummate masters of unarmed combat. When fighting bare-handed ie, without any weapons, they may add 3 points to their COMBAT SKILL.

Animal Mastery
Grand Crowns with this ability are able to plant in the mind of any animal the image of their most-feared predator or adversary. Under the influence of this illusion the animal will believe, with all of its senses, that it is being confronted by such a creature instead of a Kai Grand Crown.

Grand Pathsmanship
Grand Crowns with this skill are able to create a clear passageway through dense undergrowth, forest, or jungle. Once having passed through this

passageway, the plant material will revert to its normal state. This skill can also be employed by a Kai Grand Crown against magical foliage, or to counter any plant material ranged against him by an enemy.

Kai-screen

Grand Crowns who possess mastery of this Discipline are able to mask the goodly aura which radiates naturally from their minds and bodies. Additionally, Grand Crowns can deliberately alter these auras to give a false impression of themselves to creatures who are sensitive to such psychic auras.

Grand Nexus

Grand Crowns who possess this Discipline are able to speak a Kai Power Word – a holy utterance which will cause physical and psychic damage to any single creature within a radius of thirty feet. The degree of damage so caused, and the resultant drain upon a Grand Crown's reserves of ENDURANCE, are dependent upon individual circumstances. The power and range of this skill increases as a Grand Master rises in rank.

Kai-alchemy

Grand Masters who have reached the rank of Grand Crown are able to use the following Brotherhood spells:

Teleport – By casting this spell, Kai Grand Crowns can transport themselves physically to any place which they can see with their own eyes. The spell will carry the caster, his equipment and clothing, to his chosen sighted destination. It cannot be used on any other living creature and it will not transport any other living creature along with the caster. Use of this spell will cost the caster between 1 and 5 ENDURANCE points every time it is used. This cost reduces as a Kai Grand Master increases in rank.

See Illusion – Using this spell, a Kai Grand Crown is able to detect an illusion and know immediately its true identity or purpose.

The nature of any additional improvements and how they affect your Grand Master Disciplines will be noted in the 'Improved Grand Master Disciplines' section of future *Lone Wolf* books.

GRAND MASTER'S WISDOM

You are about to face an adversary who possesses skills and abilities commensurate with your own. Even though you have returned to Sommerlund, the land of your birth, you should remain wary and on your guard at all times. Your enemy is cunning and ruthless; you can expect no quarter from him whatsoever.

Some of the things that you will encounter during your adventure will be of use to you in this and future *Lone Wolf* books, while others may be red herrings of no real value at all. If you discover items, be selective in what you choose to keep.

Pick your four Grand Master Disciplines with care for a wise choice will enable any player to complete the quest, no matter how weak their initial COMBAT

SKILL and ENDURANCE scores may be. Successful completion of previous Lone Wolf adventures, although an advantage, is not essential for the completion of this Grand Master adventure.

May the light of Kai and Ishir be your guide as you strive to defeat the agents of Naar.

For Sommerlund and the Kai!

1

The jangle of keys and the metallic squeal of a rusty iron drawbolt makes your pulse quicken. Moments later, the heavy dungeon door creaks open and two imperious figures step with caution into the dingy cell. They are protected by a dome of radiant magical energy, yet you can see enough of their features through this shimmering force-field to recognize them to be Baron Calder and Guildmaster Banedon.

'Well met, old friend!' you call out, but Banedon does not return your greeting. His countenance is one of fearful suspicion. Clearly he and the Baron suspect you are the evil impostor who has wrought havoc across Sommerlund.

'Come now, Banedon. Truly, it is I – Lone Wolf. Won't you release me from these shackles?'

Banedon takes hold of a crystal pendant that hangs from a chain around his neck and a wave of strong psychic energy washes over you. The sensation is deeply unpleasant, but you resist the urge to use your psychic Kai defences to repel it. Instead, you allow this mental probe to access the recesses of your mind and gradually Banedon's grim expression is replaced by a smile. He nods approvingly and, in an instant, the magical barrier which protects the two men blinks out of existence.

If you possess a Platinum Amulet, turn to **195**.
If you do not possess this Special Item, turn to **302**.

2

You hit the stinking water and dive beneath the surface. But moments later you are struck forcefully in the side by the tip of the creature's tail, lifted into the air, and dashed against the rough earth wall of the cavern: lose 4 ENDURANCE points.

Coughing and gasping for breath, you find your feet and claw the muck from your eyes just in time to see the serpent's tail swishing back towards your chest. Instinctively you throw yourself against the wall and the deadly barbed tail misses you by inches. As it sweeps past, you draw your weapon in readiness to strike out at it the moment it comes within range.

Ukara (chained): COMBAT SKILL 44 ENDURANCE 45

This serpent is immune to all forms of psychic attack, except Kai-surge.

If you win the combat, turn to **348**.

3

You draw your divine blade from its scabbard and a halo of golden light irradiates the throne hall. Naar bellows with a terrible rage. He is mortally aghast that such a holy weapon should be unsheathed in his inner sanctum, and in his rage he summons yet a further horde of Crypt Spawn to attack and overwhelm you.

Crypt Spawn hordes:
COMBAT SKILL 55 ENDURANCE 40

If you win this combat, turn to **350**.

4

Using your Magnakai Discipline of Nexus, you concentrate upon a small area of the plant wall and will the fibres to loosen and tear. The wall is remarkably resilient, and you expend a great deal of energy before the tough fibres weaken and bend to your will: lose 4 ENDURANCE points.

Eventually you are able to create a large enough hole in the stem through which you can make your escape.

To continue, turn to **230**.

5

Your killing blow decapitates the head of this mechanical beast, sending it bouncing across the chamber. Fountains of fiery sparks shoot from its severed neck and its torso cracks and crumples in on itself. Within seconds, the body is transformed into a glowing mound of steel slag.

Warily you approach the creature's head and prod it with the tip of your weapon. When you are sure that it is safe, you examine it more closely and discover a curious disc of iron wedged in a crease in the back of its skull. Guided by instinct, you take this disc and insert it into the wall. Moments later, the door opens with a hiss of escaping air.

If you wish to retrieve the Iron Disc before you pass through the door, record it on your *Action Chart* as a Special Item which you carry in the pocket of your tunic.

To continue, turn to **83**.

You throw yourself to the ground and the beam of blazing white light passes within inches of your head, close enough to scorch the hood of your cloak. The moment you hit the warehouse floor, you roll over and over and scramble for the nearest cover – a heavy iron chest, banded and riveted with steel. The warrior follows your swift move and looses a second beam from his spear which slams into the iron chest with stunning force. You gasp with horror as you see the side of the chest bulging towards your face. Its thick rivets tremble and its age-blackened skin smoulders with a sullen heat. Instinct takes over, making you roll away from the iron chest and seek cover elsewhere. As you move, the beam of light tears through the rear of the iron box and destroys the ground where, only moments before, your face had been.

You call upon all of your camouflage skills to mask your body as you hurriedly seek a way to escape from this warrior and his sorcerous weapon. You reach the base of a large steel tank and scramble up a ladder fixed to its side. The top of the tank is stacked high with coiled ropes and you force yourself in amongst them. A few moments later you watch the warrior approach the smouldering remains of the iron chest. He is close enough now for you to see that his weapon is attached by a length of steel cable to a canister strapped to his back.

If you possess a Bow and the Discipline of Magi-magic, and have attained the Kai rank of Sun Lord, turn to **209**.

If you do not possess a Bow or this skill, or if you have yet to attain the rank of Sun Lord, turn to **156**.

7

Guided by a circle of blazing beacons, Javano the pilot lands the skyship expertly in the middle of a paved training park located within the castle's expansive grounds. In Tyso a curfew is in force, and the only figures lawfully abroad this night are Baron Medar's guardsmen whose numbers have been doubled by a regiment of Border Rangers recently arrived from Holmgard. Banedon suggests that you stay on board until he has informed Baron Medar of the true situation.

'The guards of Tyso are under orders to kill you on sight,' he says, as he gets ready to disembark. 'It would not be wise to show yourself, Grand Master, until I have explained all to the Baron.'

You remain in his quarters while Banedon seeks an audience with Baron Medar. Shortly he returns with the Baron who, upon entering the cabin, greets you warmly like a father welcoming home a favourite son.

'You will always be welcome here, Lone Wolf,' he says, clasping your hand in friendship. 'I knew in my heart that you were innocent of these crimes which have so shocked our people. You may rely on me to help you find this impostor who has sought to harm us and bring dishonour upon your good name.'

You thank the Baron for his support and his pledge of loyalty, and you tell him how pleased you are to be in Tyso after the months you have spent abroad.

'Then come, my lord, let's adjourn to my hall where you may enjoy the hospitality of my court,' he says, and turns to leave the cabin. As he reaches the door he says: 'Oh, and by the way, there are some men waiting there who, I'm sure, will be most pleased to meet with you.'

Turn to **238**.

8

The arrow hits your forehead, yet fortunately at an angle. It carves a gash across the top of your head and removes a deep furrow of skin and hair as it glances off your skull bone: lose 6 ENDURANCE points.

Biting back the pain, you clasp both hands to your scalp and muster your healing skills to staunch the heavy flow of blood. As you stagger to your feet, you look to the jungle and pinpoint the place where the arrow emerged. When you magnify your vision you see the face of your enemy – Wolf's Bane – partially hidden by a tree. He is laughing, his teeth showing white against the deep green of the jungle. He mouths a curse and then he springs to his feet and disappears into the undergrowth.

Determined that you are not going to allow him to

escape so easily, you break into a run and give chase.

Turn to **90**.

9

Your killing blow punctures the beast's single lung and heart, sending it swiftly to the bottom of the flooded cellar. You sheathe your weapon and strike out for the surface where, upon clambering onto the steps, you pause for a few moments to regain your composure. As you recover, you note that one of your Backpack Items is missing, lost during your underwater combat with the Ekmakon. (Erase from your *Action Chart* the item which you have recorded at the top of your list of Backpack Items.)

Eager to continue your pursuit, you climb the steps and emerge through a trapdoor into the rubble-heaped city ruins. There is no sign of Wolf's Bane, but when you hurry to where you saw him last, you discover a flight of steps leading down into a wide underground passage. His tracks can be seen clearly imbedded in the muddy floor of this tunnel.

The tunnel passes under a street and then surfaces in front of a grand two-storey building, once a busy warehouse that stored braided coils of fine copper cable. You avoid the main entrance in case your adversary is lying in ambush there, and enter instead by way of a flight of iron steps that lead to a second floor window. The moment you set foot inside the building you sense that Wolf's Bane is here. Warily you explore, your nerves stretched to breaking point as your eyes seek out detail in the darkness. You are approaching the west wing of this building when you suddenly catch sight of your opponent through a hole in the floor. He is sitting on his haunches behind a mound of wooden crates, busily eating a green-skinned fruit, and he is unaware that you are watching him.

> If you possess Magi-magic, and have attained the rank of Grand Thane (and wish to use your skill), turn to **81**.
>
> If you possess a Bow, and wish to use it, turn to **106**.
>
> If you possess Kai-alchemy, and wish to use it, turn to **319**.
>
> If you possess none of these skills, or have yet to reach the required level of Kai rank, or simply choose not to use them, turn instead to **20**.

10

The door opens with a hiss. You rush forward and immediately sidestep to place a solid wall between you and the steel monster. Then the door slides shut and, a few moments later, you feel a shudder run through the wall as the creature slams head-first into the portal and shatters its skull.

To continue, turn to **83**.

11

One of the arrows grazes your left shoulder and gouges a furrow of skin from the back of your left thigh. You stifle a cry, but the intense pain that grips your injured limbs warns you at once that the tip of the arrow was tainted with poison.

Your innate healing skills counter the poison before

it can do its deadly work, but your body's defences draw heavily on your reserves of strength and the curing process leaves you feeling weak and light-headed: lose 4 ENDURANCE points.

To continue, turn to **309**.

12

Luckily, the acid-spitter was the only one of its kind to be found lurking in this hall, and you are able to reach the door without being spat upon by one of its many brothers. The door itself is unlocked and, without further delay, you pull it open and hurry through into the hall which lies beyond.

You are hungry and, unless you possess the Discipline of Grand Huntmastery, you must now eat a Meal or lose 3 ENDURANCE points.

To continue, turn to **220**.

13

You hit the ground with a numbing jolt and almost lose consciousness. As you lie there, dazed and gasping for breath, you hear the anxious voices of your companions swirling around in your mind. You cannot move but you are able to draw on your Magnakai curing skills to staunch your bleeding wounds. Gradually you feel your strength returning. The young Kai gather around and lift you carefully to your feet. As your vision clears, you see that the doorway to the tomb is now devoid of rubble. You sense that the destructive force of the power-glyph has been discharged, but only temporarily. It is recharging, and you have but a few seconds in which to enter the tomb before the deadly device is fully active once more.

'Quickly, my lords,' you gasp, as you break free of their grasp and stagger towards the entrance, 'follow me!'

They hesitate, fearing you are about to trigger yet another explosion. 'Hurry!' you cry, 'the trap is spent but its power is fast returning. We must enter now!'

Turn to **131**.

14

You utter the words of the Brotherhood spell *Lightning Hand* and point your right hand at the onrushing beast. A tingle runs down your arm and a bolt of power bursts from your fingertip. It arcs towards the creature's head and there is a splash of hissing sparks as it rips a strip of steel from the creature's skull. But the wound is not fatal. The beast shudders under the impact yet it hardly slows its pace, and now there is no time left to launch a second bolt. You only have two seconds remaining in which to unsheathe a hand weapon, as this great metallic horror comes leaping at you through the darkness.

Mech-wulf: COMBAT SKILL 40 ENDURANCE 36

This creature is immune to all psychic attacks.

If you win this combat, turn to **5**.

15

The arrow clips the top of your right shoulder and rips away a strip of skin: lose 3 ENDURANCE points.

Wincing at the sharp pain, you clasp your left hand to the wound and use your healing skills to staunch the flow of blood. Then you get to your feet and look to the jungle to pinpoint the place where the arrow emerged. When you magnify your vision you see the face of your enemy – Wolf's Bane – partially hidden by a tree. He is laughing, his teeth showing white against the deep green of the jungle. He mouths a curse before springing to his feet and running off into the undergrowth.

Determined that you are not going to allow him to escape so easily, you rush forward and give chase.

Turn to **90**.

16

You trawl the depths of your psychic defences to construct a fortress wall to protect yourself from this agonizing mental assault. The process drains your reserves of strength (lose 5 ENDURANCE points), but the effort is not in vain. You feel your vitality returning as you force the pain from your mind.

This psychic assault has been one of the worst you have ever experienced. You have survived, but your Kai senses tell you that your ordeal has not ended. You force open your eyes and look with dread at the terrible threat that confronts you.

Turn to **300**.

17

You raise your weapon and lash out at the creature's ugly maw. You wound the beast but it only serves to make him more angry. With a jerk of his head, he spits a gout of venom which splashes the front of your tunic and rapidly melts through the cloth to attack your skin.

Pick a number from the *Random Number Table* (0=10). If you possess the Discipline of Grand Nexus, deduct 2 from the number you have chosen. The resultant score is equal to the number of ENDURANCE points you lose due to the harmful effects of this creature's highly corrosive saliva.

Before the beast can spit at you again, you strike a blow which crushes its windpipe and sends it sinking fast to the bottom of the flooded cellar. Free now to continue your pursuit, you climb the steps to emerge amongst the ruins of the city. There is no sign of Wolf's Bane, but when you hurry to where you saw him last, you discover a flight of steps leading down into a wide underground passage. His tracks can be seen clearly imbedded in the muddy floor of this tunnel.

The tunnel passes under a broad avenue and then surfaces in front of a grand two-storey building. This was once a busy warehouse that stored braided coils of fine copper cable. You avoid the main entrance in case your adversary is lying in ambush there, and enter instead by way of a flight of iron steps that lead to a second floor window. The moment you set foot inside the building you sense that Wolf's Bane is here. Warily you explore, your nerves stretched to breaking point as your eyes seek out detail in the darkness. You are approaching the west wing of this building when you suddenly catch sight of your opponent through a hole in the floor. He is sitting on his haunches behind a mound of wooden crates, busily eating a green-skinned fruit, and he is unaware that you are watching him.

> If you possess Magi-magic, and have attained the rank of Grand Thane (and wish to use your skill), turn to **81**.
>
> If you possess a Bow, and wish to use it, turn to **106**.
>
> If you possess Kai-alchemy, and wish to use it, turn to **319**.
>
> If you possess none of these skills, or have yet to reach the required level of Kai rank, or simply choose not to use them, turn instead to **20**.

18

To the left of the tunnel arch you discover two squares of opaque crimson gemstone separated by a small slot. The squares are similar in size and design to those you encountered at the entrance to the temple of Avaros. These, too, comprise a locking mechanism that controls this portal. By tapping upon each square a correct number of times you will cause the lock to disengage and the portal to rise.

You place your fingers lightly upon the squares and feel the tell-tale vibrations that are the key to deciphering the secret code. After only seconds you are able to determine that the first code is equal to the number of islands south of the Kirlundin island of Hemd.

The second code is equal to the number of villages that lie on the highway between the cities of Toran and Anskaven.

In order to discover the exact numbers that will open the portal, consult the map at the front of this book.

When you think you know the two-digit solution, turn to the entry that is the same number as your answer.

If you cannot decipher the codes, turn instead to **242**.

19

Suddenly the Bangrol shrieks in agony as a steel-tipped arrow skewers its skull. The force of the impact sends it cartwheeling through the air to crash limply against the chamber wall. You glance to your left and see a grinning Blazer calmly shouldering his bow.

'Well done, Blazer,' you say, as you sheathe your weapon. 'Your bowmanship's as keen as ever. Those many hours you've spent in the Monastery butts were not in vain, eh!' The young Kai Master smiles his gratitude for your welcome words of praise.

'Now, my lords, we must press on. We've a trail to find,' you say, and motion your companions to follow as you leave this chamber by a tunnel in its south wall.

Turn to **298**.

20

You call upon your Magnakai Discipline of Psi-surge and focus a pulse of psychic energy at the head of your mortal enemy. The moment you launch your mental attack, you see him physically shudder. Then his body stiffens and his half-eaten fruit drops from his grasp. You have hit your target, but you sense resistance; your adversary has powerful psychic defences with which he can counter your attack.

You feel a sudden wave of pain wash through you as he repels your mental assault and turns it back on you: lose 1 ENDURANCE point. To your dismay, you watch as Wolf's Bane leaps to his feet and makes a hasty escape, seemingly uninjured by your mental assault.

Turn to **224**.

21

Cautiously you approach the slain warriors. You are eager to examine their strange armour and you are particularly curious about the light-emitting spears they wielded; weapons such as these could prove useful in your fight against Wolf's Bane. However, on examining these steely shafts you discover that they are now useless. The source of their power was contained in the canisters strapped to the warriors' backs, a power that is now depleted.

When you prise open a helmet and breastplate, you discover a thin, pale-skinned humanoid within. His bone structure and muscularity is surprisingly weak for a warrior, prompting you to suspect that he must have relied heavily on his power-fed armour for strength and protection. This sallow-faced soldier has a lean and brutal appearance, a look which resembles that of an emaciated Drak-karim.

After having satisfied yourself that there is nothing worth salvaging from the bodies of these two slain enemies, you make a cursory check of your own equipment. You are hungry, and unless you possess the Discipline of Grand Huntmastery, you must now eat a Meal or lose 3 ENDURANCE points. Having satisfied your curiosity and your appetite, you hurry out of this derelict warehouse by a rear door and continue your hunt for Wolf's Bane's trail.

Turn to **31**.

22

The creature's sharp proboscis misses you by inches. Before it can strike again, you prise yourself out of the cluster and retreat back along the stamen until you are out of harm's way. Blindly the giant insect stabs and slashes, splintering stamen tips and drenching you with showers of sticky pollen. Fortunately, the span of its gigantic wings and the narrowness of the plant's corolla conspire to prevent it from reaching deeper into the plant, and you are able to escape without injury.

You retreat all the way down to the bowl of the corolla, from where you began your ascent. Looking around you see that the hollow stem is now the only remaining chance you have of getting out of this plant alive.

Turn to **103**.

23

The instant you tap in the second code the portal

begins to rise. You wait until it has risen a few feet and you are sure that no enemy awaits you on the other side, then you duck under the heavy iron plate and hurry into the tunnel beyond. As you run, you hear the portal slamming shut behind you with a dull reverberating boom.

Turn to **115**.

24

Your Kai camouflage skills keep you hidden from the unwanted attentions of these thirsty creatures, and you reach the stairs without being detected. Once you are here, you ascend to the balcony and hurry through the arch.

To continue, turn to **50**.

25

Suddenly the tip of the creature's tail erupts from beneath the water and comes swishing towards your face. Instinctively you dive to avoid being hit and ripped open by the scores of razor-sharp barbs that encircle its tail.

Pick a number from the *Random Number Table*.

If the number you have picked is 7 or less, turn to **2**.
If it is *8* or more, turn to **169**.

26

You summon your Kai skills to mask your body prior to uttering the words of the advanced Brotherhood spell *Teleport*. You focus on the distant balcony and feel yourself leave the ground and surge towards it. As you come close to passing over the fountain, you pray that your camouflage skills will keep you hidden from the eyes of the creatures gathered there.

Pick a number from the *Random Number Table*. If you possess Assimilance, add 4 to the number you have picked.

If your total score is 5 or lower, turn to **179**.
If it is 6 or higher, turn to **245**.

27

You approach the hut and crouch down beside its mud wall, close to its open door. Your senses detect no glyphs or other traps here, and there are no residues of magical energy that might betray the presence of illusions or shielding spells. However, your Kai senses do pick up a strong aura of evil lingering at the rear of the hut, close to the water's edge.

You move around to the rear of this hovel and discover that the bank is deeply undercut where the soft earth has been eroded by the fast-flowing stream. Standing in a line in the shadow of the undercut are a dozen wooden cages, each containing a fleshless skeleton. A shiver runs down your spine as your Magnakai Discipline of Divination detects the lingering agonies of these luckless victims. They suffered cruelly at the hands of the natives of this settlement before death finally ended their torment. The shock of your discovery is unnerving: lose 1 ENDURANCE point.

You leave the stream and return to the front of the hut. Inside the open doorway you discover several fruits stacked in mounds on a mat of woven rushes.

I. A huge tiger-like beast comes bounding out of the darkness ahead.

Somewhat to your surprise, your senses tell you that they are nutritious and safe to eat. (There are sufficient fruits here for 3 Meals.)

Wary of further delay, you approach the trench at the centre of the hut. Your tracking skills locate your enemy's tracks leading down the flight of steps, and quickly you follow them into an underground tunnel. You have gone only a few yards along this narrow passageway when suddenly you hear the terrifying roar of a large cat. With an abruptness that takes your breath away, a huge tiger-like beast comes bounding from out of the darkness ahead. So sudden and unexpected is this creature's attack, that you only just have enough time to unsheathe a hand weapon as it hurls itself upon you.

Rahjaz: COMBAT SKILL 48 ENDURANCE 41

This creature is immune to all forms of psychic attack, except Kai-surge and Kai-blast.

If you win this combat, turn to **249**.

28

You unsheathe the Sword of the Sun and a shimmering halo of light engulfs the blade. This golden glow washes over the rubble-strewn steps and illuminates something that, until now, had gone unnoticed.

Lying across the open doorway to the tomb is a slab of granite. Cautiously you move nearer to inspect a strange mark on its surface which is glinting in the light from your sword. You discover that it is an intricate design which has been scratched

upon its surface. Someone has gone to the trouble of smearing it with dirt and a magical spell of shielding has been placed upon it to disguise its true purpose, yet you immediately realize what it is and you recoil from the slab, hurriedly retreating a dozen paces. It is a glyph of power: a magical booby trap that has been expertly camouflaged to keep it secret. If anyone or anything were to step upon or pass over this glyph, the energy contained within it would be released in one devastating instant.

You sheathe your sword and warn the others of what you have found, telling them to retreat with you to a safe distance. From the cover of a gravestone, several yards from the tomb, you instruct Star Lynx to pick up a rock and hurl it through the open doorway. He responds by selecting an apple-sized chunk of granite which he lobs with accuracy into the tomb.

Pick a number from the *Random Number Table*.

If the number you have chosen is *1–3*, turn to
211.
If it is *4–9*, turn to **53**.

29

You climb more than two hundred steps before the staircase arrives at a short tunnel which opens into a damp, cavernous hall. This huge chamber is partitioned into pens which house several giant dragonflies, similar to those you encountered when first you arrived on Avaros. High above, great oblong sections of the steel roof are open to the elements and the bases of passing storm clouds are lit up by the glow from the hall's phosphorescent lighting. You scan the rainswept pens for sight of your adversary, and find him climbing upon the saddled back of a great crimson dragonfly. He urges the creature into the air and it obeys with stunning swiftness. You watch as Wolf's Bane steers his winged mount once around the roof of the hall, and then, to your horror, you see him bring the creature to hover directly over your head. He shouts at you, but his words are lost in the buzz of the dragonfly's massive wings. Then he leans from the saddle and casts down a metallic box before urging his mount skywards. The box lands close by, bouncing once before coming to rest near your feet. Your heart pounds when you sense that it is a powerful time bomb. A panel on the side of this device contains several illuminated numerals that are blinking intermittently. You can see by the numbers remaining that you have only 30 seconds before the bomb detonates.

If you wish to attempt to diffuse this time bomb, turn to **177**.

If you decide instead to mount one of the giant dragonflies and attempt to escape from this hall before the bomb explodes, turn to **190**.

30

Nausea wells up from the pit of your stomach as the lower chamber of the tower is suddenly transformed into a whirling spiral of violent colours and noise. You feel yourself falling forwards into this vortex and, for a few fleeting seconds, you glimpse your adversary. He is brandishing his sword and laughing like a madman, his face twisted with maniacal glee as he rides this terrifying whirlwind. Then he is lost to the chaos of the maelstrom and he vanishes from your sight.

For what seems like an eternity you spin and fall through a rainbow of colour and sound. Only gradually do you become aware that this nightmare journey is coming to an end when the noise abates and the swirling colours begin to fade. Then, with a jolt, you find yourself standing ankle-deep in stagnant green water, struggling to keep your balance. You draw your weapon and scan your surroundings, fearful of a sudden attack, but you soon realize that you are alone.

You appear to be under the ground, standing in a crude sewer-like tunnel which has been excavated by primitive means. The roots of trees protrude from its beaten earth ceiling and there is a stale and unpleasant smell of rotting vegetation. You use your psychic skills to probe for Wolf's Bane but you cannot detect his presence, and so you sheathe your weapon and relax your guard. The encounter with the manifestation of Naar has left a fear gnawing at your heart, the fear that the Dark God could at any moment he chooses lay claim to your soul. But your Kai courage swiftly overcomes the anxiety and you draw comfort from your faith in the Gods Kai and Ishir. You offer up a prayer to them to watch over you during the coming trial of strength, and vow that you will never lose hope, no matter what the dangers you may have yet to face. As if in answer to your prayer you feel a surge of energy flow through your body, revitalizing your mind and senses (restore any ENDURANCE points which you may have lost during your adventure so far).

Alert and confident, you peer along the gloomy tunnel in both directions and try to determine the best course to follow. Neither way looks especially appealing.

If you choose to explore the tunnel ahead, turn to **128**.

If you decide to follow the tunnel behind, turn to **262**.

31

The rear of the warehouse opens onto a wasteland of shattered rubble which is bisected by a dead stream of salty, acidic water. You trudge across this bleak and forbidding landscape, past sharp spires of crimson and jet that erupt through the dereliction to scratch the cloudy sky. Rust-red water encircles their bases, lending them a wholly sinister aspect.

To your eyes it seems as if this blighted city has been impaled upon these cruel, towering spikes.

Beyond the spires you discover a paved street almost clear of debris. You find several sets of footprints here, and your hopes are raised when you determine that one set belong to Wolf's Bane. You follow them to a gutted building, several storeys high, which is adorned with strangely angular gargoyles. The inside of this crumbling edifice is completely empty and your adversary's trail passes through it to a rear exit. As you emerge on the far side, you catch your first breathtaking glimpse of this grim city's tallest structure.

Turn to **250**.

32

The giant serpent tries desperately to resist your mental command to retreat, but it cannot overcome your powers of persuasion. Slowly it retreats towards the cavern wall until it is halted by the chain to which it is shackled. Cautiously you advance, keeping a wary eye on its trembling form as you skirt around the opposite wall. Within seconds you are able to reach the safety of the exit tunnel and make your escape unscathed.

Turn to **115**.

33

The water is refreshingly cold to your touch, but it has a metallic taste that makes you retch: lose 1 ENDURANCE point.

Turn to **336**.

34

Kekataag the Avenger is attired in battle armour that glimmers like slime-dulled gold. Beneath his helmet there is a hollow skull-face from which emerges a sickly stench that permeates even the foul air of this hall. The skulls and bones of humans bedeck his armoured hide and in his mighty hands he carries a great two-handed axe, its blade stained black with the blood of his countless victims.

This fearsome warrior holds you with his glowing eyes and you feel waves of powerful psychic energy buffet your mind. You muster your Magnakai defences to repel this attack, but you sustain psychic shock before your defences knit together properly: lose 4 ENDURANCE points. This sudden and unprovoked attack leaves you in no doubt that Kekataag is deeply jealous of your supposed defeat of Lone Wolf.

Turn to **255**.

35

Steel Hand and the other Kai clear away the rubble to reveal a trapdoor set into the floor. You command Star Lynx to tie one end of his rope to its bronze ring and then together, from a safe distance, you pull open this stone hatch. No traps are sprung as the heavy slab of stone creaks open, and when you move closer, you see a circular chute and a ladder descending to a deeper level of the catacombs. You peer down into the darkness and you detect fresh tracks on the ladder's iron rungs. You are back on the impostor's trail.

II. The fearsome warrior holds you with his glowing eyes.

Cautiously you lead the descent into the chute, using your powers of infravision to scan for signs of movement in the damp darkness below. After several minutes you reach the bottom of the ladder where you discover a large, vaulted chamber.

Around its walls are positioned urns and grey stone caskets, each embellished with traces of gold. There is an unexpected air of opulence about this vault which prompts you to guess that it is a secret burial tomb.

> If you have ever visited the Graveyard of the Ancients in a previous *Lone Wolf* adventure, turn to **182**.
> If you have never visited this place, turn to **206**.

36

Your target is beyond the effective range of your power word. The energy of your attack dissipates before it reaches Wolf's Bane, and all that he feels is a cool and pleasant breeze. The use of this Discipline at such extreme range drains your strength unnecessarily: lose 3 ENDURANCE points.

You watch your adversary and see him getting to his feet: he is moving deeper into the jungle. Fearing that he is getting away, you dash from the cavemouth and chase after him. But you have covered fewer than a dozen yards when suddenly an arrow comes whistling out of the undergrowth. It speeds directly towards your face with terrifying accuracy.

> If you possess Kai-alchemy, and have attained the rank of Sun Knight or higher, turn to **152**.
> If you possess Kai-alchemy but have yet to reach this level of Kai mastery, turn to **270**.
> If you do not possess this Grand Master Discipline, turn to **232**.

As your enemy's platform passes through the next level of the tower, he leaps off and disappears from view. A few moments later, when your platform reaches this level, Wolf's Bane is nowhere to be seen. You step into the circular chamber and cast your eyes around its bare metallic surfaces. There is only one exit from here: a narrow tunnel in the north wall.

Quickly you enter this tunnel and discover footprints in the dust which blankets the floor. You follow the tracks, but they soon fade and then disappear completely. You stop to examine the floor and your tracking skills tell you that your adversary is deliberately masking his trail. Determined not to give up the pursuit, you break into a run and hurry along this tunnel to where it makes a sharp turn to the left. What you see filling the corridor ahead brings you skidding to a halt.

The way is blocked by a criss-crossed tangle of thick, gluey strands, which are anchored to the floor, walls and ceiling. You sense that Wolf's Bane has cast this magical net to ensnare and delay you while he makes good his escape.

If you possess the Sommerswerd, turn to **118**.

If you possess Kai-alchemy, and wish to use it, turn to **233**.

If you possess Grand Weaponmastery, have attained the Kai rank of Sun Lord, and possess a bladed weapon (ie sword, axe, dagger etc), turn to **187**.

38

If you possess none of these skills, rank, weapons or Special Item, turn to **69**.

38

Your blow has ripped a hole in the creature's silvery wing. The wound is not fatal, but the damage is enough to render the hungry creature incapable of ascending any higher. It emits a loud buzz of frustration which fades as it slowly spirals away towards a cluster of smaller dragonflies hovering near the centre of the gorge.

Several minutes elapse before your tireless mount reaches the apex of the cavern and soars into the light-filled vent. Upon entering this vast aperture you are buffeted by crosswinds which sweep you and your air-steed precariously close to its rocky lip. The shock of the unexpectedly violent wind causes your mount to circle around the lip and attempt to dive back into the cavern. Blind with fear, it no longer responds to your commands, forcing you to take drastic action to avoid being carried back into the gorge. As you swoop past a rocky outcrop, you leap from the creature's back and abandon yourself to the crosswinds. Only your Kai mastery and your lightning-swift reactions save you from being crushed to death as you are blown towards the jagged, volcanic rock.

Miraculously, you survive the impact and are able to haul yourself out of the vent and climb safely onto a surface that you assume is the roof of the cavern. Seeking shelter from the raging crosswinds, you squeeze yourself into a hollow in the porous rock from where you are able to take stock of your new surroundings. The sight makes you gasp, for it is a view that truly rivals the fertile wonders of the cavern below.

Turn to **239**.

39

You utter the words of the Brotherhood Spell *Lightning Hand* and loose a power beam of your own at the back of the running warrior. It tears open the canister that is strapped between his shoulder blades and, with a sudden eruption of blue-white light, he is hurled upon the cylinders that cover his slain comrade. For a few seconds a spidery net of pulsating light enshrouds the two lifeless warriors, then it crackles and disappears, leaving behind an acrid stench of scorched metal and roasted meat.

Turn to **21**.

40

You step away from the body of your enemy and allow yourself a smile of grim satisfaction that you have, at last, rid Aon of this evil intruder.

'Hurry, Lone Wolf,' says Alyss, impatiently, 'Naar is vengeful. He will soon be wanting to know how his champion is faring. If he finds him slain, we will both feel his wrath.'

'Then we must escape from here,' you reply, 'but how? Do you know of a way?'

'Mmm . . . maybe,' she replies, narrowing her green eyes. 'Yes . . . I've got a plan.'

If you possess the Discipline of Kai-screen, and

have attained the rank of Kai Grand Crown, turn to **280**.

If you do not possess this skill, or if you have yet to attain this level of Kai mastery, turn to **98**.

41

Black Hawk unsheathes his sword and rests this gleaming band of Sommlending steel across his forearm, awaiting your signal to proceed. You cast your eyes over the surface of the wall one last time, to satisfy yourself that you can detect no lurking traps, and when you are fully confident that it is safe you nod your head affirmatively. Because you are so sure that there is no threat, what occurs in the next instant is doubly shocking.

Black Hawk puts the tip of his sword to the hairline crack in the wall and presses forward with all of his weight. But, unexpectedly, he meets with no resistance. His blade disappears into the wall and the young Kai Master stumbles forwards and vanishes through the seemingly solid granite. For a second or two there is a deathly silence. Then an explosion of white light obliterates your vision and you feel a searing wave of heat buffet your face and body.

Pick a number from the *Random Number Table*.

If the number you have picked is *0–4*, turn to **223**.
If it is *5–9*, turn to **99**.

42

You hear the great portal closing behind the hover-wagon. It makes surprisingly little noise for such a huge expanse of iron, barely a serpent-like hiss as it seals out the stormy city wind. You stay hidden until the wagon comes to a halt and then you venture a glance over the side of its cargo bay to assess the situation.

Before your eyes there stretches a cavernous plaza, crafted entirely of steel, glass, silver and iron. Towering girders arc over your head, buttressed upon each other to support the many upper levels of this stupendous edifice. The plaza is vast and alien in design, and it is virtually deserted. You count no more than six armoured warriors, some so far distant that you have to magnify your vision to be sure that they are what they seem.

The arrival of the wagon attracts no attention. The driverless craft has docked of its own accord at a steel jetty that encircles an iron support pillar. The coast is clear and so you waste no time in attempting to locate your adversary's trail. As expected, you find traces of his tracks close to the portal. They lead you to an archway which opens into a steel-lined chamber that has two exits: one to the left, the other to the right. Here the tracks become indistinct; you are unable to determine which way Wolf's Bane went from here.

If you wish to explore the left exit, turn to **243**.
If you choose to explore the right exit, turn to **254**.

43

You take several deep breaths as you prepare to utter the Kai power word. Focusing on your enemy's hiding place, you expel the word – *Kai!*

– and you see the undergrowth shimmer as the force of your exhalation ploughs through the jungle like an invisible fist.

Pick a number from the *Random Number Table*. If your current ENDURANCE points score is more than *20*, add *1* to the number you have picked.

If your total score is now *8* or less, turn to **36**.
If it is *9* or more, turn to **327**.

44

Your arrow flies straight and true and hits the creature's glowing eye, yet it does not penetrate deep enough to cause a fatal wound. The eye dims but the beast does not slow its pace, and there is now no time for a second shot. You only just have time to unsheathe a hand weapon to defend yourself as the metallic horror comes leaping at you through the darkness.

Mech-wulf: COMBAT SKILL 44 ENDURANCE 40

This creature is immune to all psychic attacks.

If you win this combat, turn to **5**.

45

The swift and unexpected ferocity of this psychic assault makes you fall to your knees and clasp your head in both hands. Pain is flooding your mind and causing your body to convulse with psychic shock. Dimly, through a red haze, you sense that the Platinum Amulet you are wearing around your neck affords you some defence against this attack. Sadly, it is insufficient to save you from sustaining damage to the fabric of your mind.

III. The metallic horror comes leaping at you through the darkness.

Pick a number from the *Random Number Table* (0=10). Now add *5* to the number you have chosen. The resultant total equals the number of ENDURANCE points you have lost due to this psychic attack.

If you survive this mental assault, you may continue by turning to **203**.

46

You open the cage door and command the creature to jump onto your oustretched arm. You are hoping to be able to use it as a guide to help you find Wolf's Bane, but the primate does not cooperate as expected. It is deeply confused. It thinks that you are Wolf's Bane and adamantly it refuses to leave its cage.

You detect that it has suffered cruelly at the hands of the impostor, and this sudden realization serves to strengthen your determination to find and defeat him. You take one last look at the pitiful creature before closing the cage door, and continuing your exploration of the tower by way of the circular stairs.

Turn to **287**.

47

As you emerge from the tunnel, the oppressive jungle heat hits you like a sledgehammer. Your Magnakai Discipline of Nexus automatically regulates your body temperature, making the heat bearable, yet even so it comes as a shock that any living creature can exist in this hellish environment.

Unfortunately, the shock of the jungle heat is only the first of two nasty surprises that await you. The second is a barbed arrow that whistles from out of the dense foliage and comes speeding towards your forehead!

If you possess Kai-alchemy, and have attained the rank of Sun Knight or higher, turn to **152**.

If you possess Kai-alchemy but have yet to reach this level of Kai mastery, turn to **270**.

If you do not possess this Grand Master Discipline, turn to **232**.

48

The instant you set foot into the hall, your worst fears are realized. The floor is not solid and quickly you sink up to your waist in a dry, foul-smelling quicksand. You spread your arms and legs to slow your rate of descent, but your action does little to help your situation. It seems the more you move the quicker you sink. In desperation, you attempt to swim through this dry morass.

Pick a number from the *Random Number Table*. If

you possess Grand Huntmastery, add *1* to the number you have picked. If you possess Grand Pathsmanship, add *2*. If your current ENDURANCE score is *12* or less, deduct *1*.

If your total score is now *3* or lower, turn to **158**. If it is *4* or higher, turn to **257**.

49

With mixed feelings of fear and fascination you force open your eyes and gaze upon your alien surroundings. At first it seems as if you have fallen into a humid, green-walled cell, illuminated by a solitary lantern at the apex of a fluted chimney-like ceiling. Then slowly your mind makes sense of sights and smells and the realization of where you are makes you shiver with dread.

You have landed inside the corolla tube of some gigantic flower. Huge stamens rise up to the light from the sticky bowl-shaped floor on which you lie, and nearby there is a large, chute-like tunnel which drops away into the plant's hollow stem. For a moment you close your eyes and let your psychic senses explore this strange environment. Your greatest fear is that you have been drawn through the Shadow Gate to the Plane of Darkness, the supernatural realm of Dark God Naar, yet you can detect no abnormally high concentrations of evil. Also, you are unable to sense the presence of your adversary – Wolf's Bane. Your hopes begin to rise when suddenly you realize that you are still somewhere within the material universe of Aon. You are able to determine that this alien place is not your home world, yet you are certain that it is a planet that lies within the same galaxy as Magnamund.

You cling to this small crumb of comfort and resolve to find a way of returning to Magnamund as quickly as you can. You open your eyes and stare around the walls of your plant-prison, searching for a means of escape. There appear to be only two ways out: by climbing a stamen towards the light high above, or by sliding down the nearby chute which plunges deep into the plant's stem.

If you wish to climb a stamen, turn to **264**.

If you choose to slide down the hollow stem, turn to **103**.

50

You have covered twenty yards of a passageway that extends from the balcony when you hear a grating noise. It is a concealed portal, and it is sliding shut to seal off the hall through which you have just passed.

Ahead lies a chamber which is bedecked with a score of lavish tapestries, each depicting the landscapes of remote and wondrous planets within the universe of Aon. Your adversary's tracks pass through this opulent chamber and end at a pair of stout wooden doors, inlaid with exquisite gold marquetry. You place your ear to one of the doors and concentrate. The only sound you can hear is the crackle of a log fire, but your Kai senses detect the presence of your adversary in the room beyond. You peer through a keyhole and glimpse part of a gallery with a railed parapet. The wooden rails are lit from below by the warming yellow flicker of a fire.

You reach out to open the doors and confront your

enemy, but a strong sense of unease stays your hand. It feels as if a swarm of butterflies are fighting to escape from your churning stomach. You have a chilling premonition that a confrontation with Wolf's Bane in the room beyond could prove fatal for both of you. This fear prompts you to pray to the Gods Kai and Ishir to sustain and protect you in the coming fight.

Pick a number from the *Random Number Table*.

If the number you have picked is *0–4*, turn to **104**.
If it is *5–9*, turn to **216**.

51

You relax the tension in your body and allow yourself to enter a trance state, the preliminary stage required before you spirit-walk. You feel yourself leave your corporeal body and, in spirit form, you move through the curtain of vines and out into the jungle heat. Immediately beyond the cave mouth there is a small clearing which slopes away to the jungle perimeter. You scan the border of dense foliage and you are shocked when you detect your adversary, Wolf's Bane, hiding among the bushes less than fifty yards away. He is armed with a bow which he has trained upon the entrance to the tunnel.

You retreat into the cave mouth and re-enter your body. On awakening from your trance, you move forward and peer through the hanging vines to locate your enemy's hiding place. So advanced is his camouflage skill that it takes you several minutes to find him. Once you are sure you have him, you allow yourself a smile; you are looking forward to turning the tables on this arrogant impostor.

If you have a Bow and wish to use it, turn to **196**.

If you possess Grand Nexus, and have attained the rank of Kai Grand Crown (and wish to use your mastery), turn to **43**.

If you do not have a Bow, the Discipline of Grand Nexus, or if you have yet to attain this higher level of Kai mastery, turn to **114**.

52

You haul yourself out of the putrid, salty water, and narrowly avoid the clutches of the cellar beast. The creature opens its fanged jaw and issues a gurgling roar of frustration as it gets ready to climb onto the steps and pursue you.

If you possess Grand Pathsmanship, and have attained the rank of Sun Thane, turn to **172**.

If you do not possess this skill, or if you have yet to attain this level of Kai mastery, turn to **17**.

53

Star Lynx dives for cover behind the gravestone, but you stay on your feet to watch the trajectory of the rock as it disappears into the open tomb. The moment it passes over the glyph there is a blinding flash of white light, followed almost instantly by the deafening crackle of exploding electrical energies. You are hit by the concussive force of the explosion which knocks you flat on your back – lose 2 ENDURANCE points.

As you lie on the hard damp ground, gasping for breath, you can hear splinters of stone ricocheting off the surrounding gravestones and smell the stench of scorched· earth and ozone in the air. Then, abruptly, the noise and light abates and the burial ground is shrouded once more in gloomy silence. You pull yourself to your feet to see that the doorway is now clear of rubble, save for the slab upon which the glyph is inscribed. The destructive power of the glyph has been discharged, but only temporarily. Your senses warn you that it is recharging; you have but a few seconds in which to enter the tomb before the magical device is active once more.

'Quickly, my lords,' you shout, as you hurry towards the entrance, 'Follow me!'

Turn to **131**.

54

One of the arrows whistles past dangerously close to your legs, while the other passes wide and shatters harmlessly against the ceiling. Before the creatures can reload and fire again, you reach the balcony and speak the words which negate the effects of the *Teleport* spell. The moment your feet touch the ground, you hurry into the archway beyond.

Use of the *Teleport* spell costs you 4 ENDURANCE points. Be sure to make the necessary adjustment to your *Action Chart*.

To continue, turn to **50**.

55

Cursing your predicament, you steel yourself to

confront the chained serpent. Unsheathing your weapon, you take your first tentative steps towards the hissing creature and soon discover that its iron collar and chain will prevent it from reaching you so long as you keep close to the cavern wall. Mindful of this, you skirt around the writhing serpent and inch your way carefully towards the tunnel. However, you have progressed only a few yards when you feel the floor sloping away. The water is getting deeper.

If you possess Magi-magic, turn to **234**.
If you do not possess this Grand Master Discipline, turn to **25**.

56

Your adversary sniggers when he hears your cry of pain. Yet, despite the burning agony of your wound, you wrench the evil shaft from your chest and force yourself to stand. Defiantly, you level your weapon at the darkened stairwell. But Wolf's Bane is no longer crouching near the steps; he is fast ascending them. Calling upon your innate healing skills, you staunch the flow of blood that is soaking the front of your tunic and stumble towards the staircase in pursuit of your hated foe.

Turn to **29**.

57

You place your lips to the plant wall and utter the power word of the Elder Magi: *Gloar!*

The explosive power of this magical word is greatly accentuated within the confines of the stem. It tears a large ragged hole in the plant wall through which, with little difficulty, you are able to make your escape.

Turn to **230**.

58

Hurriedly you recite the words of the Brotherhood spell *Counterspell* and, to your relief and amazement, the fire-bolt splutters and dissolves within an arm's reach of your face.

Turn to **37**.

59

Guided by your advanced Kai instincts, you avoid the rain of debris without too much difficulty and reach the entrance to the skull-rock unscathed. Without any hesitation you enter the misty portal in pursuit of your enemy. Barely seconds later, there is a tremendous explosion and the entire temple ceiling collapses.

Turn to **174**.

60

The moment you twist the dial to the correct number, the panel slides open and a rush of air surges into the cell. Greedily you fill your lungs as you stagger out into the corridor and make your way back along this steel-lined passage towards the stairs. Quietly cursing your ill luck, you descend the steps to the foyer and leave the building.

Turn to **71**.

61

Using your advanced mastery, you are able to project the image of the creature's most-feared adversary into its mind's eye. The huge serpent reacts violently; it twists and wrenches at its iron collar in a desperate attempt to break free from its bonds. Its great body, which is studded with tiny barbed horns, thrashes the water into a stinking foam as it writhes back and forth in front of the exit tunnel. Your psychic projection has this creature terrified, but its state of near-panic will now make it difficult for you to reach the tunnel and escape from this cavern.

If you possess Kai alchemy, turn to **293**.
If you do not possess this skill, turn to **326**.

62

The moment you negate your spell of levitation and set foot upon firm ground, you feel a warm breeze. You sense that it comes from a stairwell at the far end of this new hall and, when you investigate it, you rediscover Wolf's Bane's footprints on the stone steps. You cast your hands over them and detect that this is not a false trail: your enemy passed this way sometime within the last hour.

Slowly you ascend the stairs and arrive at the arched entrance to a large, vaulted stone chamber. Gathered around a fountain set into its north wall are a group of six grey-skinned humanoids. They are busy drinking a clear, oily fluid that pours from the fountain's spout into a semi-circular trough. All are barefoot and clad in rags, and they are each armed with a spear and a bow. The only exit from this chamber appears to be an archway set high in the north wall. There is a balcony in front of it that can only be reached by two flights of stairs which rise up on either side of the fountain.

Quietly you observe the creatures slaking their thirsts, and you try to formulate a way in which you can get past them and reach the balconied exit in the north wall.

If you possess a Bow, and the Discipline of Magi-Magic, and have attained the rank of Kai Grand Guardian, turn to **138**.

If you possess Kai-alchemy and have attained the rank of Grand Crown (and wish to use it), turn to **26**.

If you do not possess these skills, or a Bow, or if you have yet to attain the required levels of Kai mastery, turn to **121**.

63

You release your grip of your enemy and roll away from him. Moments later, the beam from his comrade's weapon hits his side and erupts through the back of his armour. The force of the impact lifts him bodily from the floor and hurls him into a pile of rusty cylinders, bringing them crashing down to bury him. Shocked and angry at having accidentally killed his confederate, the newly-arrived warrior rushes forward. He is determined to find and finish you once and for all, but his anger and his armour put him at a disadvantage. He fails to see where you have gone and, under cover of the smoke and debris, you manage to circle around behind him without being seen.

If you possess Kai-alchemy, turn to **39**.

If you do not possess this Grand Master Discipline, turn to **349**.

64

The moment you complete the code, you feel a shuddering vibration run through the great iron portal. Slowly it grinds open to reveal an antechamber that is lit by a dozen flaming torches set around its glassy walls. The wind has now become so fierce that it is tearing the fabric of your cloak and tunic. Rather than remain outside in the storm a moment longer, you hurry through the open portal and seek shelter within.

Turn to **227**.

65

It takes you more than half an hour to cut a clear path through these magical strands, and the effort leaves you aching with fatigue.

Pick a number from the *Random Number Table*. If the number you have picked is *0–4*, reduce your ENDURANCE score by 2 points. If the number you have picked is *5–9*, reduce your ENDURANCE score by 4 points.

To continue, turn to **316**.

66

You ask Steel Hand to give you his rope and he obeys dutifully. Then you utter the words of the Brotherhood Spell *Levitation* and almost immediately you feel gravity losing its grip on your body. Gently you rise to the ceiling of the vault where, using the exposed stone buttresses, you are able to pull yourself along until you are directly above the centre of the fissure. Here you fix one end of the rope to an exposed stone beam and cast the other end to your companions waiting below. One by one they swing across the void and, when all have crossed safely, you untie the rope and pull yourself to the far side before intoning the words that cancel the effects of the spell.

It is clear from their wide-eyed expressions that they are all impressed with your mastery of Brotherhood magic, especially Steel Hand. You gather up his rope and as you give it back to him you say: 'Don't worry. One day I'll instruct you in the ways of magic so that you, too, can walk a ceiling!'

The young Kai Master smiles as he stuffs his rope into his bulging backpack.

'And now, my lords, we must press on. We've a trail to find,' you say, and you motion your companions to follow as you get ready to leave this chamber.

Turn to **160**.

67

You feel your throat tightening and your lungs collapsing as the air is sucked out of the chamber. The whirling flames of the fire have rapidly transformed into a raging vortex which is dragging into its core every loose item in the banquet hall. You and Alyss hang on to the banister rail affixed to the gallery stairs, but it is becoming increasingly difficult to maintain your grip. Chairs, tapestries, tables and other furniture batter you as they tumble past to be sucked into the vortex (lose 4 ENDURANCE points). Then the rail collapses and the two of you are drawn into the raging heart of this fearsome whirlpool.

Turn to **170**.

68

So advanced is your adversary's camouflage skill that it takes you several minutes to locate him, despite the fact that he is less than fifty yards away. He is partially hidden behind a tree, and he is armed with a bow which is trained upon the entrance to the tunnel. Once you are sure you have found him, you allow yourself a smile; you are looking forward to turning the tables on this arrogant impostor.

If you have a Bow and wish to use it, turn to **196**.

If you possess Grand Nexus, and have attained the rank of Kai Grand Crown (and wish to use your mastery), turn to **43**.

If you do not have a Bow, the Discipline of Grand Nexus, or if you have yet to attain this higher level of Kai mastery, turn to **114**.

69

The strands of this magical net are thick, sticky and tough. Clearing a way through them quickly becomes a trial of strength and stamina.

Pick a number from the *Random Number Table*. If you possess a bladed weapon, add 3 to the number you have picked.

If your total score is now 4 or less, turn to **65**.

If it is 5 or more, turn to **228**.

70

You are within a few feet of the exit tunnel when a heavy sheet of iron falls from the ceiling and seals off your chosen route of escape. You spin around and glimpse the creatures in the pot who attempted to shoot you full of arrows. They are small, blue-skinned reptilians, with cruel crocodilian faces and curiously human hands. They are armed with finely crafted bows of gleaming white bone which you detect are capable of discharging six poisoned arrows every second. The reptilians are close to reloading these bows – you must act quickly if you are to avoid becoming the target of another deadly volley.

> If you possess Kai-alchemy, and wish to use it, turn to **277**.
> If you possess Magi-magic, and wish to use it, turn to **219**.
> If you possess a Bow and wish to use it, turn to **136**.
> If you possess neither of these Disciplines, or a Bow, or choose to use none of them, turn to **82**.

71

Once outside, you focus your tracking skills and attempt to pick up your enemy's trail. You have a feeling that he may have doubled-back on his tracks and so you retrace your steps to the street where you first appeared in this alien city. As you are nearing this place, you suddenly hear the ringing metallic clang of an iron girder falling from a height. The noise echoes from an alleyway off to your right and immediately you go to investigate.

At the end of the alley you discover a derelict warehouse. Fire has ravaged its interior and much of the roof has caved in, but amongst the debris you can see that it once stored metal cylinders and coils of wire. You stop at the entrance and listen. Your caution is rewarded when you hear footsteps at the rear of the building. You draw your weapon and enter, using the debris for cover as you inch your way towards the back of the ruined warehouse. You are moving between cover when suddenly you see the outline of a human form silhouetted against a broken window. Instantly you know that it is not Wolf's Bane: this figure is clad in grey, close-fitting armour and is holding a metallic spear. The realization makes you hesitate, and in that split second of indecision, the armoured figure sees you and raises its spear. A blinding flame ignites at its tip and a beam of white-hot light comes speeding towards your chest.

Pick a number from the *Random Number Table*. If you possess Grand Pathsmanship, add 3 to the number you have picked.

If your total is now 5 or less, turn to **312**.
If it is 6 or higher, turn to **6**.

72

You motion to your companions to follow, then you take your first step into the dark tomb. Suddenly there is a blinding flash of white light followed almost instantly by the deafening crackle of exploding electrical energies. Pain consumes your body as you are lifted into the air and thrown backwards by the blast. You have triggered a hidden power-glyph, a magical booby trap, and you have been caught by its explosive energy.

Pick a number from the *Random Number Table* (0=10). Now add 5 to the number you have picked. The resulting total equals the number of ENDURANCE points you lose.

> Make the necessary adjustments to your *Action Chart* before turning to **13**.

73

Your advanced Kai mastery reveals to you that a hoard of precious platinum is stored in a chamber at the end of the left corridor.

> If you wish to explore the left corridor, turn to **95**.
>
> If you choose instead to explore the right corridor, turn to **137**.

74

The creature that is diving towards you suddenly freezes in mid-air. The morbid fear of death that had gripped your heart quickly evaporates, but you are left with a feeling of deep unease as your senses detect that something extraordinary is taking place around you. The hall has become filled with a deadly silence and everything, including the tongues of flame trailing from the creature's sword, and the blazing fire in the grate, is utterly frozen. It is as if time itself is standing still.

Wolf's Bane is a frozen statue, his face fixed in the malevolent sneer he was wearing in gleeful

IV. Armed with only a mischievous grin, Alyss sees off Wolf's Bane's winged minion.

anticipation that you were about to meet your doom. You are beginning to think that perhaps you have been killed and that this is life after death, when suddenly you glimpse a blurred movement out of the corner of your eye.

From the shadows cast by the gallery there steps a young teenage girl. She is dressed in a leather jerkin and threadbare trousers which are cut short at the knees. She is barefoot and appears to be armed only with a mischievous grin.

'Who . . . who are you? Why are you here?' you stammer, dumbly. Casually she walks towards you and reaches up to touch a finger to the frozen fiery sword clutched in the taloned hands of Wolf's Bane's winged minion. There is a gentle *Pop!* and the creature disappears.

'I'm Alyss, and I do hate cheats,' she says, as she wanders over to where Wolf's Bane is standing immobile. Cheekily she pokes out her tongue at him and then she spins on her heel to face you.

'Now, perhaps you can finish what you came here to do, Lone Wolf,' she says, and claps her hands three times. A sudden rush of noise assails your ears and your senses reel as the reality of time comes flooding back into the hall.

Turn to **296**.

75

With a loud and angry buzzing noise, the predatory dragonfly circles you twice and then dives down like a speeding hawk to make its initial attack.

Golasyx: COMBAT SKILL 49 ENDURANCE 45

This creature is attempting to stab you with the tip of its spear-like proboscis as it swoops past, therefore you need only fight this combat for one round.

> If you inflict an equal or greater ENDURANCE loss upon the enemy in this single round of combat, turn to **163**.
>
> If you sustain a greater ENDURANCE loss than your enemy, turn to **221**.

76

Using your advanced mastery, you cause the dragonfly's wounds to close up and heal. Consciousness and strength return to its battered body and the creature is able to pull out of its dive before it is too late. It swoops deep into the cavernous moat of the tower to gather speed for its ascent into the clouds. As you soar past the top of the tower, you see that the dragonfly pens have been completely destroyed by the explosion. Fire rages through the uppermost levels of the tower, and is spreading quickly to those below.

Turn to **310**.

77

You use your tracking skills to find your enemy's trail, but following it becomes increasingly difficult. You sense that he has used magic to assist his escape for the foliage hereabouts is entangled far tighter than in neighbouring areas of this jungle. Your progress is slowed, but eventually you reach a copse of toa trees where you hear the sound of running water away to your left. Your adversary's tracks turn in this direction and you follow them all the way to the banks of a fast flowing watercourse.

Less than fifty yards downstream there is a primitive settlement of huts that form an untidy line along the edge of the stream. The tracks appear to lead to this settlement but you can see no sign of Wolf's Bane. The place looks deserted.

> If you wish to stay in the jungle and observe the settlement, turn to **215**.
> If you choose to continue your pursuit, you can approach the settlement under cover of the jungle, by turning to **297**.

78

You motion your companions to follow as you leave this chamber by a tunnel in its south wall. This new passage gradually descends by slope and stair through deeper levels of the catacombs. You detect no trace of the impostor and, when eventually the tunnel comes to a dead end, you curse your ill luck and turn reluctantly to retrace your steps. It is then that you sense a faint but lingering aura of evil close to the tunnel floor.

Closer inspection reveals a trapdoor set into the flagstones. You pull this heavy hatch open and discover a circular chute and a ladder descending into darkness. Your heart misses a beat when you notice fresh tracks on the ladder's iron rungs: at last you have found the impostor's trail.

Cautiously you lead the descent into the chute, using your powers of infravision to scan for signs of movement in the damp darkness below. After several minutes you reach the bottom of the ladder where you discover a large vaulted chamber. Around its walls are positioned urns and grey stone caskets, each embellished with traces of gold. There is an unexpected air of opulence about this vault which prompts you to guess that it is a secret burial tomb.

If you have ever visited the Graveyard of the Ancients in a previous *Lone Wolf* adventure, turn to **182**.

If you have never visited this place, turn to **206**.

79

You make your way towards the avenue and take cover in a darkened alleyway, an ideal place from which to observe the passing traffic. Thirty minutes elapse before a hover-wagon glides into view at the city end of the avenue. It is bound for the tower, but you note that its cargo compartment is completely sealed and so you decide to let it pass and wait for a more suitable target. Fortunately, you do not have to wait too long. Within the space of a few minutes another appears. This one, like the first, has no driver, but its cargo bay is open to the elements. As you wait for it to get closer, you judge its speed and prepare yourself to leap aboard as it passes. It is less heavily laden than the first wagon and is moving much quicker; leaping aboard this speeding wagon is not going to be easy.

Pick a number from the *Random Number Table*. If you possess the Discipline of Grand Pathsmanship, add 3 to the number you have picked. If your current ENDURANCE points score is 12 or less, deduct 2 from the number you have picked.

If your total is now *2* or less, turn to **301**.

If it is *3* or higher, turn to **185**.

80

The grating rumble.of heavy stone on stone heralds the sudden appearance of the impostor. Like some secret door to a nightmare realm, the entire far wall of this vault is slowly sliding open. Violent tremors shake the floor and orange tongues of flaming gas shoot from the ever-widening gap. Silhouetted in the centre of this fiery portal is a warrior clad in a parody of the robes of a Kai Grand Master. His stature and his facial features bear an uncanny resemblance to your own, yet the two of you are not entirely identical. The eyes of this impostor betray his true nature for they are black and cold; they are like two tiny windows through which you can see the evil lurking deep within his heart.

The portal crackles and roars like a blazing furnace yet it radiates no heat. You sense powerful magic at work here and you shout a command to your young Kai comrades to prepare themselves for combat. They react as one, their years of training suppressing their fears, and swiftly they draw arms and form up in a protective circle around you. The impostor unsheathes his black-bladed sword and gives vent to a chilling laugh that momentarily drowns the roar of the flames. His cruel laughter fills your head and suddenly the stone walls of the vault seem to writhe and buckle inwards. Your psychic Kai defences resist this illusion and the distortion ceases, yet as it does so you realize that something important has changed. You command your companions to retreat towards the chute but they do not respond. They are completely rigid, frozen immobile like four stone statues.

'Ha ha ha . . . ' cackles the impostor, 'so we meet at last, Lone Wolf.' He advances a little nearer and you feel an icy chill wash over you. The body of this bogus Kai lord radiates coldness.

'How I have enjoyed myself in your guise,' he sneers. 'Let me introduce myself . . . I am Wolf's Bane. An apt name don't you think?'

'What is your purpose?' you growl in reply, your hand poised to draw a weapon in case he should attempt to launch a sudden attack.

'Why, I've come to kill you, of course,' he retorts, his voice full of contempt. 'There should be but one Grand Master and only I am worthy of such distinction.' The impostor narrows his coal-black eyes and curls back his lip in disdain.

'And I intend to prove my worthiness, Lone Wolf,' he adds, with quiet menace.

'How so?'

'By a duel,' he replies. 'I challenge you to a duel. A fight to the finish. A fight between just you and I, Lone Wolf.'

'And if I refuse your challenge?' you retort, defiantly.

'Then your four frail acolytes will die.' The impostor sweeps his sword in a wide arc, as if to emphasize his threat, and the fiery wall at his back begins to change. The plumes of flame twist and spin with increasing speed until the wall is transformed into

V. 'Why, I've come to kill you, of course,' retorts Wolf's
Bane in contempt.

a swirling vortex. Fear tightens its icy fingers around your throat as you witness the creation of a Shadow Gate – a portal to another plane of existence. At once you know his threat is real. If he were to direct the power of the vortex towards your paralysed companions, they would be helpless to resist. They would be sucked into the Shadow Gate and destroyed.

'Very well,' you say, 'I accept your challenge.'

Wolf's Bane gives a triumphant smile and whirls his black sword around his head. Then he dashes the blade to the floor and, in a terrifying instant, a mighty gust of wind tears the two of you off your feet and sends you both hurtling into the fiery heart of the dread Shadow Gate.

Turn to **200**.

81

You focus on Wolf's Bane as you intone the words of the Old Kingdom spell *Hold Enemy*. You see him shudder, and the half-eaten fruit drops from his grasp. But suddenly you sense resistance: your adversary is casting a counterspell. There is an abrupt release of energy as the effects of your spell are negated and broken: lose 1 ENDURANCE point.

To your dismay, you watch Wolf's Bane leap to his feet and make a hasty escape.

Turn to **224**.

82

The reptilians complete the reloading of their bows, and together they lean over the lip of the pot to take aim at your unprotected body. Simultaneously they let fire, sending a stream of arrows whistling towards your chest, and you are forced to dive headlong into the grey slime to avoid being peppered with poison-tipped shafts. One of the bone arrows clips your calf and you feel an agonising pain shoot up the back of your thigh as its poison enters your blood: lose 2 ENDURANCE points.

Your innate healing skills quickly neutralize the venom and seal the wound. Dripping with slime, you scramble to your feet and hear your thwarted enemies cursing you vilely as they fumble with their bows.

If you possess a Naptha Bomb, turn to **288**.
If you do not possess this item, turn to **320**.

83

The steel walls of the room you have entered are sheened with ice. Several tall glass canisters stand in a circle at the centre of this frigid chamber, connected to one another with pipes and coils of copper cable. Their liquid contents bubble and seethe and appear to be boiling despite the freezing air temperature. You walk around them, mesmerized by the strange beauty of the roiling multicoloured fluids. Then you sense imminent danger somewhere to your right and instantly you spin around to face it, your hand reaching reflexively to the weapon at your belt.

You see a dark stairwell and a shadowy shape which is crouched near to the bottom steps. It is Wolf's Bane. He is clutching a bow and he has an arrow drawn ready to fire. The instant you see him he releases his bowstring and the tip of the arrow bursts into flames as it comes speeding towards your chest.

Pick a number from the *Random Number Table*. If you possess Grand Huntmastery, add 2 to the number you have picked. If your current ENDURANCE score is 10 or less, deduct 2.

If your total is now *3* or lower, turn to **155**.
If it is *4–7*, turn to **102**.
If it is *8* or higher, turn to **248**.

84

You increase the rate of your ascent and swiftly accelerate beyond the reach of the predatory dragonfly. Unable to catch you, it emits a loud buzz of frustration which slowly fades as it spirals away. You glance down to see it satisfying its appetite in an attack upon a number of smaller dragonflies. From this great height they appear to be no larger than a cluster of colourful dots hovering above the centre of the great gorge.

After several minutes you reach the apex of the cavern and soar into the light-filled vent. Upon entering this vast aperture you are buffeted by crosswinds which sweep you precariously towards its rocky lip, yet your Kai mastery and your lightning-swift reactions save you from being crushed to death as you are blown onto its jagged, volcanic edge.

You survive the impact and are able to haul yourself out of the vent and climb safely onto a surface that you assume to be the roof of the cavern. Seeking shelter from the raging crosswinds, you squeeze yourself into a hollow in the porous rock from where you are able to take stock of your new surroundings. The sight makes you gasp, for it is a view that truly rivals the fertile wonders of the cavern below.

Turn to **239**.

85

'Surely the great master of all the Kai is not a coward?' sneers Wolf's Bane, taunting you for your refusal to accept his challenge. 'Are you not brave enough to prove your worth?'

'I have no fear of you, impostor,' you retort. 'I simply do not trust you to fight with honour.'

'If you should win the duel, Lone Wolf, you will be returned to Tyso – of that you have my word. And the word of my master.'

'Both equally worthless,' you reply, coolly.

For a few moments you stare into your adversary's murderous eyes and sense that every word of his pledge is a lie. Yet you know that your options are limited. If you do not fight this duel, he will be sure to summon his minions to capture and kill you. There is nothing to gain by refusing his challenge and so, with reluctance, you accept.

Turn to **304**.

86

The arrow soars over your shoulder and lodges itself in the tangle of vines that hang down in front of the cave mouth. You spring to your feet and swiftly your sharp eyes pinpoint the place where the arrow emerged from the jungle perimeter. When you magnify your vision you see the face of your enemy – Wolf's Bane – partially hidden by a tree. He is cursing you, his teeth showing white against the deep green of the jungle. Then he sees that you have spotted him and he turns and runs, quickly disappearing into the dense undergrowth.

Determined that you are not going to allow him to escape so easily, you rush forward and give chase.

Turn to **90**.

87

Swiftly you place an arrow to your bow and take aim at the beast's left eye. It senses a threat to its sight, and instantly a layer of interlocking metal plates emerges from beneath its protruding forehead to protect its vision. You offer up a prayer to the God Kai to guide your aim, for the moving target you are attempting to hit is now no wider than the edge of a coin.

Pick a number from the *Random Number Table*. If you possess Grand Weaponmastery with Bow, add 5 to the number you have picked.

If your total score is now 4 or less, turn to **322**.
If it is 5–9, turn to **44**.
If it is 10 or higher, turn to **299**.

88

Caldar removes his hand from his sword and heaves a sigh of relief. 'Thank Ishir you've returned to us, Grand Master. Perhaps now the evil that has befallen Sommerlund will be avenged.'

The Baron summons his gaoler who unlocks the shackles that encase your wrists. Then, as the three of you hurriedly ascend from the castle dungeons to the Great Hall, Caldar and Banedon confirm the account of events that you extracted earlier from the gaoler. In addition to these facts you also learn that several days ago an angry mob, composed in the main of soldiers and citizens from Holmgard, marched upon the Kai Monastery. Firestone, the most senior of the New Order Kai, pleaded with the mob for calm. Fortunately they heeded his call and allowed him to send four Kai Masters to Tyso – the city where the impostor was last sighted. Firestone has ordered these four Kai to track down and slay the impostor as quickly as possible.

You are in no doubt that this impostor is a formidable enemy, one who could easily prove more than a match for the four young Kai. Anxious for their safety, you request that you be allowed to ride to Tyso to join with them. Banedon is in agreement, but he suggests a swifter and surer way that you may reach Tyso. Moored to the tower of Baron Caldar's castle is *Cloud Dancer* – the Guildmaster's skyship – which he places at your disposal. Gratefully you accept his generous offer.

You are keen to leave for Tyso without further delay, but before you depart, Baron Caldar offers you the chance to equip yourself with weapons and stores from his well-stocked armoury.

If you wish to accept the Baron's offer, turn to **149**.

If you decide to decline his offer, turn to **260**.

89

Despite your valiant efforts, you are unable to revive your mount and it dies of its wounds before reaching the ground. Unfortunately, you become entangled in its trailing wings and are unable to save yourself before the giant dragonfly smashes into the rim of the moat surrounding the tower. Death is mercifully swift.

Sadly, your life and your duel end here.

90

You force your way through the dense tangle of plants and grasses and soon reach the place where Wolf's Bane lay in wait for you. The foliage around this hiding place has been carefully arranged, which suggests to you that he must have spent some considerable time setting his ambush. Yet there is also evidence of a hasty retreat. Lying on the ground behind a tree you discover 2 Arrows and a Dagger (if you wish to take one or more of these, remember to make the appropriate adjustments to your *Action Chart*).

Determined to stay on his trail while it is still fresh, you leave this hide and press deeper into the jungle in pursuit of your enemy. However, you have penetrated less than twenty yards into the undergrowth when his trail becomes indistinct.

> If you possess the Discipline of Grand Pathsmanship, and have attained the rank of Kai Grand Crown, turn to **246**.
> If you do not possess this skill, or if you have yet to attain this level of Kai mastery, turn to **77**.

91

Luckily, this acid-spitter has emptied its sac of corrosive venom and you are able to make good your escape from the hall without being spat upon as you leave. You reach the door and discover it is unlocked. Without hesitation, you pull it open and hurry through into the hall beyond.

Turn to **220**.

92

The broken buttress and the rope plummet into the fissure and are lost when they hit an underground river far below. Steel Hand swings one-handedly from the ceiling yet he manages to maintain his grip, despite being showered with loose rocks and dust. You command him to return and he obeys readily.

As soon as Steel Hand is back on solid ground, you praise his skill and his brave effort. Only ill luck thwarted him. He offers to try again but you say that it is your turn – he has already proved his courage. Blazer offers you his rope and you accept it, then you walk along the edge of the fissure until you reach the wall. You find it easy to ascend the rough surface and work your way across to a point directly above the fissure. From here you fix the rope to a secure beam and cast the other end to your companions waiting below. One by one you watch them swing across the void and, when all have crossed safely, you untie the rope and make your way over to the far side to join them.

'Come, my lords,' you say, as you jump effortlessly

down from the wall, 'we must press on. We've a trail to find.'

Turn to **160**.

93

You try to evade the crackling light that speeds towards you from the muzzle of the warrior's spear, but the wounds and fatigue you have sustained conspire to dull your reactions. You are hit in the side by this white-hot beam and hurled high into the air. Suddenly an explosion of white light obliterates your senses and, in a horrifying instant, the light that is your life is snuffed out.

Tragically, your life and your duel with Wolf's Bane ends here.

94

Using your Grand Mastery skills, you conjure a fog from the surface of the slime which rapidly fills the lower level of the vault. You hear the angry, rasping voices of the creatures echoing inside the pot as they curse the fog which is obscuring their view of the vault floor. Under cover of the vapour, you enter the vault and wade silently through the slime towards the far exit. You have just passed beneath the pot when suddenly a volley of bone arrows comes whistling down from above.

Pick a number from the *Random Number Table*. If you possess Grand Huntmastery, add 2 to the number you have picked.

If your total score is now 6 or less, turn to **11**.
If it is 7 or higher, turn to **266**.

95

This passage ends at a door crafted from sheeted silver inset with circles of iron. It has no handle and there appears to be no lock. You try pushing against it but to no avail: it refuses to open. Then you notice a small slit cut into the frame of the door and, when you run your fingers across it, you detect the tell-tale vibrations of an electrical lock.

If you possess an Iron Disc, turn to **159**.
If you do not possess this Special Item, turn to **143**.

96

You muster your psychic defences and construct a wall around your mind to protect yourself from this agonizing mental assault. Your strategy is effective, although the effort it requires depletes your reserves of strength (lose 3 ENDURANCE points).

This psychic assault has been one of the worst you have ever experienced. You have survived, but your Kai senses tell you that your ordeal has not ended; it has only just begun. You force open your eyes and look with dread at the terrible threat confronting you now.

Turn to **300**.

97

One of the arrows grazes your right forearm and gouges a furrow of skin from the top of your right thigh. You stifle a cry, but the intense pain that grips your injured limbs warns you at once that the tip of the arrow was tainted with poison.

Your innate healing skills counter the poison before it can do its deadly work, but your body's defences draw heavily on your reserves of strength and the curing process leaves you feeling weak and light-headed: lose 4 ENDURANCE points.

To continue, turn to **70**.

98

'Come, Grand Master. You're going home,' she says, and she takes you by the hand and leads you to the middle of the banquet hall, to a place directly opposite the great fireplace. 'But first we must make preparations for the journey.'

Alyss then proceeds to remove an amulet from around the throat of your slain adversary. She presses it into your palm and tells you to put it on immediately. (Record this Special Item on your *Action Chart* as a Wolf's Bane Amulet, which you wear on a chain around your neck. You must discard another Special Item in its favour if you already possess the maximum permissible.)

Having done as she requests, she then touches her finger to the two amulets that you now wear, and she smiles.

'Good, good,' she enthuses, 'these baubles will take care of you.'

She then takes a piece of limestone from her pocket and proceeds to draw a pentagram on the floor of the hall. She has half-completed the complicated design when suddenly she becomes agitated.

'Must hurry,' she mumbles, 'must, must hurry.'

Suddenly the fire in the hearth flares brightly. The flames begin to grow and whirl and slowly change colour.

'It's no good!' cries Aylss, tearful with frustration. Angrily she casts her chunk of crumbling limestone at the roaring flames and then leaps to her feet and comes rushing to your side. 'It's too late!' she screams, her voice now barely audible above the unnatural crackling of the fire, 'Naar is summoning his champion!.'

Pick a number from the *Random Number Table*.

If the number you have picked is 0–4, turn to **273**.
If it is 5–9, turn to **67**.

99

The shockwave from the blast sends you tumbling backwards into the chamber. Moments later something heavy falls across your legs, pinning you to the ground. You reach down to pull yourself free and discover that the object that is lying across your legs is Black Hawk. Dazed and trembling, you roll his limp body over and then hurriedly check to see if he is still breathing. Thankfully you discover that he is alive, although he has sustained serious injuries. His hand and sword arm are badly burnt and he is in a state of deep shock.

Using your Magnakai curing skills, you are able to stabilize his condition and bring him out of shock (in doing so you expend 3 ENDURANCE points). As you help him to his feet you look around and see that the others have been knocked flat by the blast. They too are now struggling to pull themselves to their feet. Fortunately their physical injuries are minor; their innate Kai skills appear to have spared them from serious injury. However, you sense that your inability to detect that the wall was an explosive illusion has taken its toll on their confidence.

'Our prey is far more cunning than I feared,' you say, reproachfully, 'but we are Kai and we shall rise to the challenge. Our enemy possesses strong magic and he is capable of masking it well. Yet he chooses to use it to wound and weaken our party, not to kill us. Why this should be I do not know. But from now on we cannot entirely trust our senses to protect us. We must proceed with the utmost caution.'

Beyond where the illusory north wall once stood, you can now see a small antechamber which is wreathed in acrid blue smoke. Gradually this smoke dissipates to reveal a shallow plinth upon which lies a bronze urn. This heavy object rests on its side and a quantity of pale grey ash has spilled from its hinged lid. Cautiously you approach the urn and see that there is an inscription engraved on its side. From this ancient script you learn that the ashes are the last remains of Baroness Garrulen, the wife of Hul – third Baron of Tyso. Glinting half-buried in the ash, you notice a ring encrusted with crimson gemstones (if you wish to keep this Ruby Ring, record it on your *Action Chart* as a Special Item).

You are righting the urn on its plinth when you hear Steel Hand calling you. He has found something among the rubble which litters the floor at the rear of the antechamber.

Turn to **35**.

100

You are eager to confront your enemy, but you are wary of walking into a trap. At first glance he appears to be alone in this circular hall, but then you notice something curious about the hall itself. At the four points of the compass there are rails attached to the walls. Small horizontal platforms are attached to these rails and they move along them in a continuous procession. At the north and the south these platforms ascend through holes in the ceiling; at the west and east the platforms descend through similar holes and continue through other holes cut in the floor. You suspect them to be elevators and your suspicions are confirmed when suddenly an armoured warrior appears; he is standing on a descending platform and he passes through the hall and continues travelling downwards to a level somewhere below.

Wolf's Bane is standing with his back to you and is examining a panel of glass set into the chamber wall. You magnify your vision and you see that the panel displays an illuminated view of the avenue that approaches the tower. Your adversary is watching and waiting for your approach; clearly he is unaware that you have already gained access to the tower.

Suddenly, something alerts him to your presence and he spins on his heel, his dark eyes blazing with a mixture of fear and loathing. He sees you at the entrance to the hall and immediately he leaps upon a rising north platform in an attempt to escape from you. Determined not to let him get away again, you enter the hall and jump onto a rising south platform. As the platform passes through the ceiling of the hall, it carries you up a tall open shaft. Wolf's Bane is on the far side of the shaft wall, some twenty feet above. You can see his face peering over the lip of the platform on which he is standing. He mouths something that you suspect is a curse, but then he points at you with an extended hand and a crackling arc of crimson fire leaps from his fingers and comes twisting down the shaft towards your face.

If you possess the Sommerswerd, turn to **341**.
If you do not possess this Special Item, turn to **153**.

101

You detect several footprints in the loamy mulch, all of them virtually identical to your own. They have been partially covered by leaves and there are many narrow channels in the soft soil, made unmistakably by human fingers. Your suspicions are immediately aroused; the tracks are so poorly concealed, it is as if someone wanted you to find them.

If you possess Telegnosis, turn to **51**.
If you do not possess this Grand Master Discipline, turn to **258**.

102

You throw yourself forwards to avoid the missile, yet it dips in mid-air and carves a furrow across your shoulder blades as you slide along the frost-encrusted floor: lose 5 ENDURANCE points.

Your adversary sniggers when he hears your cry of pain. Yet, despite the burning agony of your wound, you scramble to your feet and level your weapon defiantly at the darkened stairwell. But Wolf's Bane is no longer crouching near the steps – he is fast ascending them. Calling upon your innate healing skills, you staunch the blood that is trickling freely from your back and hurry towards the staircase in pursuit of your hated foe.

Turn to **29**.

103

You lower yourself carefully into the hollow stem and soon discover that it drops away very steeply.

It is a vertical tube for most of its length, yet you are able to slow your rate of descent by grabbing hold of tiny tendrils which protrude from the lining of the stem wall. As you get nearer to its base, the stem wall becomes semi-transparent and slick with moisture. You press your face to this warm surface and you are able to discern other stems. They look like the trunks of trees in a dense green forest. Then you look down to see that the stem of this plant is descending into darkness. The darkness begins at the point where the stem passes below ground level. You decide to stop at this point for you have no desire to explore the roots of this strange flower.

Carefully you examine the fabric of the semi-transparent stem. If you can force your way through this tough plant wall, you will be able to escape from your prison-like tube.

If you possess a bladed weapon, or a bladed Special Item, turn to **332**.

If you possess Kai-alchemy and wish to use it, turn to **279**.

If you possess Magi-magic and wish to use it, turn to **57**.

If you possess none of the above, or choose not to use them, turn to **4**.

104

In response to your prayer, you feel a warming sensation radiating through your body and your mind, leaving you physically and mentally refreshed and alert: restore 4 ENDURANCE points.

Confident that the divine Gods of Good are

watching over you in this moment of truth, you throw open the doors and stride boldly into the hall beyond.

Turn to **240**.

105

Having weighed the risks and options, you decide to make a dash for the exit on the far side of the vault. You are confident that the combination of surprise, speed, and camouflage will be enough to see you safely across the vault before your would-be ambushers have a chance to react to your presence.

Taking a deep breath, you launch yourself into the vault. You have covered barely ten feet of the floor when you hear the angry, rasping voices of the creatures echoing from inside the hanging cauldron. You are passing beneath this iron pot when suddenly a volley of bone arrows comes whistling down from above.

Pick a number from the *Random Number Table*. If you possess Assimilance and Grand Huntmastery, add 2 to the number you have picked.

If your total score is now *8* or less, turn to **97**.
If it is *9* or higher, turn to **180**.

106

Silently you unshoulder your bow and notch an arrow to the bowstring. Then, with cold precision, you take aim at the back of your enemy's head and release your arrow. A split second before the shaft reaches its target, Wolf's Bane senses danger and throws himself to the floor. The fire-hardened tip of your deadly missile pierces his thigh, wounding him badly, but not so as to prevent him from wrenching the shaft from his leg and making a hasty escape.

Turn to **207**.

107

This narrow passageway leads to a vault littered with scraps of cloth, rodent skins, bones, and twisted clumps of dry vegetation. Out of this carpet of debris a crude, nest-like hollow has been fashioned. The glint of burnished gold prompts you to investigate the nest more closely and, to your surprise, you discover a valuable Gold Cup (Special Item) entangled among its twigs and grasses.

Suddenly you sense movement directly overhead. You glance upwards and find yourself looking into a brick-lined vent which ascends all the way to the surface. Descending this chimney at an alarming speed is a Bangrol – an acquisitive and aggressive breed of Sommlending sea-eagle. This particular bird is far from pleased that you have disturbed its secret nest.

If you possess Animal Mastery, turn to **139**.
If you do not possess this skill, turn to **217**.

108

As you emerge from the cave mouth, the oppressive jungle heat hits you like a battering ram. Your Magnakai Discipline of Nexus automatically regulates your body temperature, making the heat bearable, yet even so it comes as something of a shock that any living creature can exist in this hellish environment.

Unfortunately, the shock of the jungle heat is only the first of two nasty surprises that await you. The second is a barbed arrow that whistles from out of the dense foliage and comes speeding towards your forehead!

If you possess Kai-alchemy, and have attained the rank of Sun Knight or higher, turn to **152**.

If you possess Kai-alchemy but have yet to reach this level of Kai mastery, turn to **270**.

If you do not possess this Grand Master Discipline, turn to **232**.

109

You follow this torchlit tunnel as it snakes through the dungeon levels of this strange castle. A growing presentiment warns you that danger lies ahead and you pause to focus your Kai skills in an attempt to determine its exact nature. You cannot identify the threat, save that it is not a living entity.

You draw your weapon and advance more cautiously now. As you turn a bend in this meandering passageway, a warrior appears from out of the gloom ahead. He is sheathed in plate armour and he clutches a sword and, at first sight, appears to be human. It is not until he steps a little closer that you see he has no neck: his visored helm hovers inches above his breastplate and is not connected to his torso.

A pulse of green light illuminates the warrior's visor and suddenly a wave of powerful psychic energy hits you with terrific force.

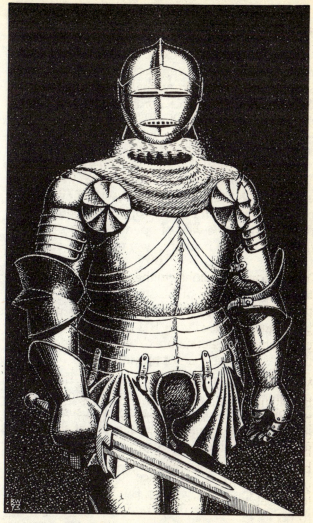

VI. The armoured warrior's head hovers inches above his
breastplate.

If you possess Kai-screen, turn to **181**.

If you do not possess this Grand Master Discipline, turn to **265**.

110

You attempt to subdue the giant serpent using your Magnakai Discipline of Animal Control, but the creature is resilient to mental suggestion and it resists your psychic command.

You are now faced with a dilemma. In order to escape from this cavern you must either face the chained serpent in combat, or you can evade it by discovering some way of opening the portcullis so that you can go back the way you have come.

If you choose to face the creature in combat, turn to **165**.

If you decide to attempt to open the portcullis, turn to **171**.

111

Alyss commands you to leave at once. The cocoon of light that surrounds her and the Moonstone is beginning to flicker with every blow it sustains from Kekataag's mighty axe. You sense that she cannot maintain her shield for very much longer.

You heed her cry and race towards the swirling mouth of the Shadow Gate. But Naar is determined to launch one last desperate attempt to prevent you from escaping. You are within ten paces of the gate when two rubbery-limbed horrors emerge from the smoky walls and hurl themselves upon you.

2 Cryopedeans: COMBAT SKILL 38 ENDURANCE 32

If you win this combat, turn to **350**.

112

The fabled Moonstone was created many thousands of years ago by the god-like Shianti, whose presence upon Magnamund heralded the dawn of humanity. This wondrous artifact contains the combined might of all their magic and wisdom, the sum of all their knowledge. So significant was the creation of this artifact that all time on Magnamund is measured from the date of its creation. It had long been held that the Moonstone's location was a secret known only to the remnants of the Shianti, who dwell upon the Isle of Lorn in deepest Southern Magnamund, yet the evidence of your eyes tells you that this mystical stone of power has fallen into the hands of the Dark God.

Suddenly the significance of the Moonstone becomes clear. Naar is using its legendary powers to generate Shadow Gates within the world of Magnamund, at locations and times of his own choosing. Such power has enabled him to send his loathsome champions to your home world, while the goodly forces of Kai and Ishir are held at bay, helpless to counter them. Only you and your Kai brethren have stood in the way of the onslaught of Naar's agents since the demise of his Darklords.

The hideous form of the Dark God returns to the dais and settles there uneasily. Then a deep rumble fills the throne hall; it is the prelude to the voice of Naar.

'You have done well, my champion,' it booms.

'Now I command you to return to accursed Sommerlund and finish my work. Prepare the way for my armies of night. At last this planet is mine for the taking. My victory is complete!'

It is clear from his words that Naar is convinced that you are his champion – Wolf's Bane – freshly returned from a duel in which Evil has triumphed. Suddenly you see Alyss emerge from the smoky wall less than a dozen paces behind Naar, yet the Dark God appears unaware of her presence. She appears calm and focused, and you sense that she is waiting for an auspicious moment to approach the plinth and take the Moonstone. With bated breath you watch as she inches closer and closer to the legendary stone. Then Naar shifts his gruesome bulk and she freezes.

'Your return to Sommerlund will not be alone, Wolf's Bane. Kekataag the Avenger will accompany you. He has a mission of assassination to complete in Toran, at the Brotherhood of the Crystal Star.'

Then the Dark God emits a high-pitched whistle and, moments later, a fearsome warrior answers the call. He emerges from the smoky wall and the floor shudders as he strides to the centre of the throne hall.

If you possess Kai-screen, turn to **183**.
If you do not possess this Grand Master Discipline, turn to **34**.

Frantically you shout the words of the Old Kingdom Battle spell *Shield* and make a swift circle in the air with your right hand. The crackling fire-bolt explodes against an invisible barrier which you have hurriedly brought into existence, and dissolves away in a shower of crimson sparks which are sucked into the depths of the shaft.

Turn to **37**.

114

You call upon all of your Kai camouflage skills to keep you hidden as you attempt to slip out of the tunnel unseen. However, your adversary has disciplines comparable to your own. He is watching the cave mouth like a hawk and your stealthy exit may not go unnoticed.

Pick a number from the *Random Number Table*. If you possess Assimilance and Grand Pathsmanship, add 3 to the number you have picked.

If your total score is now 5 or less, turn to **108**.
If it is 6 or higher, turn to **191**.

115

You follow the tunnel as it ascends towards the surface. A dot of daylight appears in the distance which, as you climb towards it, becomes a cluster of bright sunbeams filtering through a curtain of vines. This fringe of emerald streamers conceals the cave mouth entrance to this tunnel. The tunnel itself becomes increasingly humid as you get nearer to the exit. Its dry earth floor has gradually transformed into a slick and treacherous surface which is alive with beetles and centipedes, some as long as daggers.

Upon reaching the cave mouth, you stop to peer

through the hanging vines. Outside, in the fiercely tropical heat, you can see a dense jungle sweltering beneath a blazing sun. It extends in every direction towards a jagged horizon of volcanic mountain peaks. Then your eye is caught by something small and metallic glinting in the mulch of vegetation that carpets the entrance. You pick it up and discover that it is a brass button, engraved with a sun motif. It is identical to the buttons which adorn your own tunic, none of which are missing. You deduce that it has come from the tunic of your adversary, but you cannot be sure whether it was lost accidentally or was placed here deliberately for you to find.

If you wish to search the entrance for further clues to the whereabouts of your enemy, turn to **101**.

If you choose to leave the tunnel and explore the jungle beyond, turn to **47**.

116

You regard the distant vent with trepidation. It looks to be so high and so far away that you fear an escape from this world may truly be impossible. In your growing despair, you call upon your divine mentor – the God Kai – for inspiration and, as if in answer to your prayer, you experience a sudden moment of revelation in which a bold plan takes form in your mind's eye.

Using your innate Magnakai Discipline of Animal Control, you focus on one of the smaller dragon-flies that is circling above the fecund blossoms lining the lip of the gorge. Instantly it responds to your silent command and comes soaring down to land in a nearby clearing. Like a tame and obedient

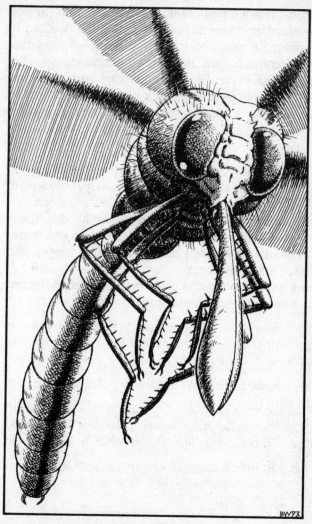

VII. The Golasyx attempts to stab you with its spear-like
proboscis as you draw your sword.

horse, this winged creature waits patiently for you to clamber upon its back. Then, once you are in position, it takes to the air with such speed that your stomach feels as if it has been physically torn from your body. Several minutes pass before you fully recover from the shock of the stunningly swift take-off, and are able to sit back and enjoy the spectacular aerial views of the gorge.

Using your palms and your knees, you quickly discover that you are able to steer the dragonfly towards the distant vent. Unfortunately, your ascent does not go entirely unnoticed. You are close to a mile above the canyon when suddenly your insectile steed attracts the unwanted attention of a larger predatory dragonfly. This predator is bigger and faster than your encumbered mount and, as it circles around him, it is clear that it is simply biding its time, awaiting the best moment to strike.

You draw your weapon and tighten your grip on your mount's scaly back as the predatory dragonfly swoops down to make its initial attack.

Golasyx: COMBAT SKILL 49 ENDURANCE 45

This creature is attempting to stab you with the tip of its spear-like proboscis as it swoops past, therefore you need only fight this combat for one round.

If you inflict an equal or greater ENDURANCE loss upon the enemy in this single round of combat, turn to **38**.

If you sustain a greater ENDURANCE loss than your enemy, turn to **192**.

117

Nimbly you dodge aside and avoid being hit by this creature's drool. At first you think nothing of it, but then you look to see where it landed and you notice that this trail of saliva is melting the flagstones.

> If you wish to attack the creature that attempted to spit acid in your face, turn to **141**.
> If you choose to evade this creature, turn to **91**.

118

Vigorously you attack the sticky strands of the net with your magical sword, cleaving through them with unexpected ease. They shrivel at the touch of your golden blade and drop in smouldering heaps onto the floor of the tunnel. Within a matter of seconds you have cut your way through and are able to continue your pursuit.

Turn to **316**.

119

You and the others watch as Steel Hand slings his coil of rope over his shoulder and commences his climb. The rough wall of this vault offers many handholds and he is able to progress swiftly to the ceiling and work his way across to the middle of the chamber, directly above the fissure. Whilst holding himself in position with his left hand, he attempts to fix one end of the rope around an exposed stone beam with his right. On completing the task he ties off the rope and tugs it to make sure it is secure. There is a loud *crack!* and you gasp with horror as the buttress to which he has fixed his rope suddenly crumbles and breaks away from the ceiling.

Pick a number from the *Random Number Table*.

If the number you have chosen is *0–7*, turn to **92**.
If it is *8* or *9*, turn to **268**.

120

At the end of the passage you discover another tunnel that leads off to the left. The walls and ceiling of this adjacent passageway are dripping wet, indicating that it passes directly under the stream. You stride along its narrow confines, your shoulders grazing the muddy walls as you advance up a flight of steps which lead to an archway supported by thick wooden beams. Beyond the arch lies a large subterranean chamber that is daubed and decorated with runes and evil insignia. It is a primitive temple and it radiates an aura of evil so vile and malicious that the thought of entering makes your skin crawl.

On the far side of this unholy place, you see a stone altar standing before a huge boulder that has been crudely chiselled to resemble a grinning human skull. An eerie green glow pulsates from the eye sockets of this great skull-rock, and a mist swirls from its open jaw. Wolf's Bane stands before the altar, an arrogant sneer spreading slowly across his face.

'I'd expected better sport from you, Lone Wolf,' he chides. 'You disappoint me . . . but no matter. Such easy triumph proves the worthiness of my master's cause. I bid you farewell, Lone Wolf. A final farewell.'

And with these chilling words ringing in your ears, your enemy stretches out both of his hands and takes hold of two iron staves that protrude from the ground on either side of the skull-rock's jaw. He jerks them out of their settings and casts them into the centre of the temple. Then, with a patronising salute, he turns and enters the open jaw, swiftly disappearing into the swirling mist.

The dull boom of an explosion somewhere in the rock above the ceiling makes your heart miss a beat. Moments later, the walls begin to shake and the floor shudders violently beneath your feet, throwing you off balance. Rock and earth cascade from the roof and fissures tear open the ground. With fear running ice cold in your veins, you begin a desperate race to reach the mouth of the skull-rock before the entire roof collapses and you are buried alive in this doomed temple.

Pick a number from the *Random Number Table*. If you possess Grand Huntmastery, add 2 to the number you have picked. For every level of Kai rank you have so far attained, above the rank of Sun Knight, add 1.

If your total score is now 3 or less, turn to **222**.
If it is *4–6*, turn to **321**.
If it is *7–9*, turn to **205**.
If it is *10* or higher, turn to **59**.

121

You detect that the fluid which the creatures are drinking is highly flammable. Armed with this knowledge, you realize that if you were able to set fire to the fluid in the trough, it would cause such a panic among the creatures that, in the ensuing chaos, you would very likely be able to reach the distant archway without being seen.

If you possess Kai-alchemy, turn to **292**.
If you do not possess this Discipline, or if you choose not to use it, turn to **314**.

122

The sudden and unexpected ferocity of this psychic assault makes you fall to your knees and clasp your head in both hands. The pain is worming its way deep into your mind, causing your body to convulse with psychic shock. Dimly, through a red haze, you sense that the Platinum Amulet you are wearing around your neck affords you some defence against this attack, although it cannot protect you completely.

Pick a number from the *Random Number Table*. For every level of Kai mastership that you have attained above the rank of Kai Grand Guardian, add 1 to the number you have picked. (The maximum you are permitted to add is 7.)

If your total score is now *3* or less, turn to **16**.
If it is *4–9*, turn to **96**.
If it is *10* or higher, turn to **315**.

123

As you retreat a few paces from the shrieking horde to unsheathe a weapon, you glance towards the plinth to see how Alyss is faring. She has drawn upon her powers to create a cocoon of energy to protect both her vulnerable body and the legendary Moonstone. Kekataag assaults this glowing shield with maniacal ferocity, his great two-handed axe drawing fiery sparks with every mighty blow. You can sense from the hatred which blazes in his supernatural eyes that he and Alyss are old enemies.

Her bravery inspires you to fight like a demon to reach the Shadow Gate and escape to your home world. You are determined that her efforts to save you will not be in vain.

Crypt Spawn horde:
COMBAT SKILL 50 ENDURANCE 36

If you win this combat, turn to **350**.

124

The great portal closes behind you with little noise, save the serpent-like hiss of escaping air. Inside, a cavernous plaza awaits you, crafted entirely of steel, glass, silver and iron. Towering girders arc over your head, buttressed upon each other to support the many upper levels of this stupendous edifice.

The plaza is vast and alien in design, and it is virtually deserted. You count no more than six armoured warriors, some so far distant that you have to magnify your vision to be sure that they are what they seem to be. Your arrival goes unchallenged and you waste no time in attempting to locate your adversary's trail. As expected, you find traces of his tracks close to the portal. They lead you to an archway which opens into a steel-lined chamber that has two exits: one to the left, the other to the right. Here the tracks become indistinct and you are unable to determine which way Wolf's Bane went from here.

If you wish to explore the left exit, turn to **243**.
If you choose to explore the right exit, turn to **254**.

125

You instruct your Kai comrades to search the chamber's four walls for hidden levers or secret panels, while you busy yourself with a careful examination of Baron Garrulen's sarcophagus. You attempt to lift its heavy stone lid but without success; it is sealed tight by the grime of centuries. You are considering ways to prise it open when Black Hawk discovers something unusual about the north wall. He signals to you to come and take a closer look.

Your experienced eye immediately detects two faint hairline cracks in its granite surface. They run vertically from the floor to the ceiling and appear to reveal the outline of a secret panel.

'Good work, Black Hawk. I'd wager the impostor escaped this way,' you say, as you scan the entire wall for some means of opening the secret panel. When no obvious way can be found, Black Hawk volunteers to force it open.

If you decide to allow Black Hawk to attempt to force open the secret panel, turn to **41**.
If you choose to try and open it yourself, turn to **286**.

126

One arrow passes wide and shatters against the ceiling. But the other shaft clips your left leg and opens a painful gash above your knee: lose 2 ENDURANCE points.

On reaching the balcony you speak the words which negate the effects of the *Teleport* spell, and, the moment your feet touch the ground, you hurry into the archway beyond.

Use of the *Teleport* spell costs you a further 4 ENDURANCE points. Remember to make the necessary adjustments to your *Action Chart*.

To continue, turn to **50**.

127

You unsheathe a hand weapon and brace your back against the door as the great metallic beast comes leaping through the darkness with its iron jaw set wide.

Mech-wulf: COMBAT SKILL 50 ENDURANCE 45

This creature is immune to all psychic attacks.

If you win this combat, turn to **5**.

128

The damp subterranean tunnel meanders for nearly a mile before entering a cavern which is lit by rays of insipid sunlight, permeating through holes in its root-entangled ceiling. Your natural pathsmanship warns you that the slimy water is deep at the centre of this cavern and, as you enter, you take extra care where you tread.

Thirty yards opposite there is a sloping tunnel which appears to ascend towards the surface; dim light illuminates its dry earthern floor. You approach it, keeping near to the cavern wall to avoid the deep water, but you have only taken a few paces when a sudden noise jars your nerves. With a dull boom, a concealed portcullis falls from the ceiling to seal off the tunnel through which you have come. Moments later, swirling eddies form in the water at the centre of the cavern and, with a hissing splash, a huge snaky head breaks through the surface and rises up to scrape the ceiling. Around its banded neck there is a collar of iron which is attached to a heavy chain. The chain disappears below the surface, keeping the creature a prisoner of this cavern. You gasp as you look into the eyes of this gigantic serpent for they radiate waves of evil that seem to place a chill in your very soul.

If you possess the Discipline of Animal Mastery, and have attained the rank of Kai Grand Crown, turn to **61**.

If you possess Animal Mastery, but have yet to attain this rank, turn to **208**.

If you do not possess Animal Mastery, turn to **110**.

129

You step away from the bodies of your slain enemies and collapse against the wall of the vault, gasping for breath. As you slowly recover, you notice that one of the reptilians has a leather pouch slung around its neck. You kneel down and tear open the pouch to discover that it contains a small Iron

VIII.   The eyes of the gigantic serpent radiate waves of evil,
chilling you to your soul.

Disc. A cursory search of his dead companion reveals a Dagger, a Sword, and a small stone phial containing a Black Potion (properties unknown).

The size and shape of the disc suddenly triggers an image in your memory. You take the disc and insert it between the gemstone squares which operate the portal lock. There is an audible *click!*, and the disc reappears at the slot (if you wish to keep this Iron Disc, record it on your *Action Chart* as a Special Item). Seconds later, the heavy portal begins to rise. You wait until it has risen a few feet and you are sure that no enemy awaits you on the other side, then you duck under the iron plate and hurry into the tunnel beyond. As you run, you hear the portal slamming shut behind you with a dull reverberating boom.

Turn to **115**.

130

The moment you key-in the correct number, it activates the detonator lock and the bomb ceases to function. You wipe a trickle of sweat from your brow as you look at the illuminated display, for it shows that there were only five seconds to go before the bomb would have exploded. Carefully you set the device down on the floor and then hurry to the nearest dragonfly pen where you use your Magnakai Discipline of Animal Control to subdue its hostile occupant. The creature reluctantly submits to your will and allows you to climb upon its back. It has no saddle, and so you are forced to grip its scaly spine as you urge it skywards in pursuit of Wolf's Bane.

As you emerge through the open steel roof of the tower, you catch a fleeting glimpse of the rainswept city far below. Then, in the next instant, you plunge into the base of the thick black storm clouds which keep this alien city forever in shadow.

Turn to **310**.

131

The inside of the tomb is a cold and sombre place, devoid of all life. Its featureless walls glisten with rivulets of moisture and the air is dank and evil-smelling, like the breath of some cold-blooded reptile. At its centre, where one would have expected to find the remains of the nobleman who long ago was incarcerated here, there is instead a yawning shaft. An ancient bronze ladder is fixed to the shaft wall which descends to an unknown depth.

Using your Kai senses, you scan the tomb and detect lingering traces of the impostor. His trail leads directly to the ladder. After satisfying yourself that your quarry has left behind no unwelcome surprises, you step onto the ladder and begin a slow descent into the shaft.

The ladder ends inside a larger stone chamber, one hundred feet below the tomb. Here you discover a granite coffin embellished with runes and ancient Sommlending script. As you wait for your Kai companions to complete their descent, you read enough of the script to learn that you have found the final resting place of Hul Garrulen, the third Baron of Tyso. Your senses confirm that you are on the trail of the impostor, yet there appear to be no other exits from this chamber, other than the shaft by which you entered.

> If you possess Kai-alchemy, and have attained the rank of Kai Grand Crown, turn to **290**.
>
> If you do not possess this skill, or if you have yet to attain this level of Kai Grand Mastery, turn to **125**.

132

You draw your divine blade from its scabbard and a halo of golden light irradiates the throne hall. Naar bellows with a terrible rage. He is mortally aghast that such a holy weapon should be unsheathed in his presence, in his inner sanctum, and in his anger he summons a host of rubbery-limbed horrors from the smoky walls of his evil domain.

> If you wish to fight these creatures, turn to **201**.
>
> If you wish to attempt to evade them by entering the Shadow Gate, turn to **162**.

133

Your eagle eyes pinpoint the place where the arrow emerged from the jungle perimeter and, when you magnify your vision, you see the face of your enemy – Wolf's Bane – partially hidden by a tree. He laughs, his teeth showing white against the dark green of the jungle, and then he springs to his feet and disappears into the undergrowth.

Determined that you are not going to allow him to escape so easily, you break into a run and give chase.

Turn to **90**.

134

Cursing your luck, you abandon the lock and turn to face the metal beast. The creature is loping towards you now, the rhythmic squeal of its metal joints counterpointed by the whirring clack of its great iron jaw. You bite back your fear and brace yourself as the beast gets ready to pounce.

If you possess a Bow, and wish to use it, turn to **87**.

If you possess Kai-alchemy, and wish to use it, turn to **14**.

If you do not possess this weapon or skill, or choose not to use them, turn to **127**.

135

The gigantic insect detects movement where it is expecting none and immediately it senses a threat to its safety. Swiftly it retracts its proboscis and rises several feet, taking its vulnerable belly beyond the reach of your sword arm. It hovers motionlessly for a few seconds, its glinting fly-like eyes watching you intently, then it emits a high-pitched shriek and at once you know that it is getting ready to attack.

If you possess Animal Mastery, and wish to use it in an attempt to repel this creature's imminent attack, turn to **178**.

If you do not possess this Discipline, or if you choose not to use it, turn to **311**.

136

With stunning grace and swiftness, you unshoulder your bow and let loose two hastily aimed arrows at the reptilians. Yet, despite the haste of your shots, both shafts find their mark. They skewer the horny skulls of these cold-blooded ambushers, killing them both in an instant. (*Remember to reduce your total number of arrows by 2.*)

Free now from the immediate threat of attack, you shoulder your bow and turn to examine the sealed portal for a lever or some other means to make it rise.

Turn to **202**.

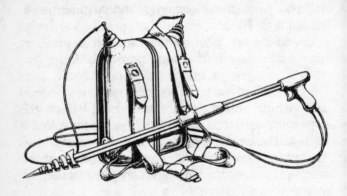

137

This passage ascends by a slope to a chamber that is lined with sheets of a glassy, jet-black mineral. A flight of iron steps ascends from here to a landing where a circular stair continues the ascent to the levels above. On a shelf beside the opening to the circular stairway there is a steel cage containing a small primate. It reminds you of the kakarmi, the wild primates who inhabit the forests around the Kai Monastery. This creature seems to recognize you, and as you approach the stairs, it begins to shriek with fear. Rather than risk drawing unwanted attention to yourself, you use your innate skills of animal control to calm and subdue the frightened creature.

> If you wish to release this creature from its cage, turn to **46**.
> If you choose to ignore it and continue on your way up the circular stairs, turn to **287**.

138

You detect that the fluid which the creatures are drinking from the fountain is highly flammable. Armed with this knowledge, you place an arrow to your bow and take aim at the stone trough. Moments before you release your bowstring, you utter the words of the Old Kingdom battle spell *Flameshaft* and the tip of your missile flares brightly with a crackling magical flame. You launch the arrow and watch as it arcs into the trough. With a deafening *wumph!*, the liquid ignites to form a blazing fireball which greedily consumes the creatures who are gathered around the lip of the trough.

> Turn to **204**.

139

Hurriedly you focus your Discipline at the attacking bird and command it to stop.

Pick a number from the *Random Number Table*. For every level of Kai rank that you have attained above the rank of Kai Grand Guardian, add 1 to the number you have chosen.

> If your total is now 7 or less, turn to **241**.
> If it is *8* or higher, turn to **307**.

140

The moment you pass into the mouth of the skull-rock you are engulfed by a dense fog that is icy-cold and impenetrable to your sight and senses. You strain your Kai skills to aid your pursuit of Wolf's Bane, but all to no avail; this ivory-white fog hides everything, swamping and distorting all sense of time and direction.

You keep moving, forcing yourself onwards even though the surface beneath your feet has become viscous and uncertain. After what seems like an eternity spent wandering through this cloudy limbo, you gradually feel the ground hardening and sense that the impenetrable fog is beginning to dissipate. Patches of grey appear in the creamy whiteness. Then the fog dissolves completely and you find yourself standing in the middle of a rubble-strewn street, surrounded by the bleak and derelict dwellings of a decaying, alien city.

It is the dead of night and a fine drizzle falls from a storm-laden sky, dampening this dreary landscape. Everywhere you look you see the hollow shells of buildings. They are heaped with mounds of broken stone, twisted rusty iron, and shattered glass. There are no trees, no blades of grass, no animals here. Everything is cold, grey, and dead.

Suddenly you sense a blur of movement beside a mountain of rubble which blocks the end of the street. You focus upon it, magnifying your vision to penetrate the damp gloom, and you are rewarded with a fleeting glimpse of Wolf's Bane. He is running away. You hurry after him and, as you crest the mound, you see him entering the shattered entrance to a three-storey dwelling close by.

Turn to **324**.

141

You draw your weapon and climb the rickety shelves in order to be able to reach this elusive acid-spitter. Despite its ungainly shape, it proves to be adept at evading your first few blows until you manage to corner it at the far end of the top shelf.

Caq: COMBAT SKILL 32 ENDURANCE 20

This creature is immune to all psychic attacks.

If you win the combat, turn to **328**.

142

Your killing blow decapitates the Bangrol and the two sundered halves of its body fall limply to the debris-strewn floor. Hurriedly you wipe clean your weapon and re-sheathe it, then you motion your companions to follow as you leave this chamber by a tunnel in its south wall.

Turn to **298**.

143

Unable to open this portal, you turn around and retrace your steps back to the junction and then explore the other passageway.

Turn to **137**.

144

Hurriedly you retreat back along the stamen until you are out of harm's way. Blindly the angry Solyx stabs with its proboscis, splintering stamen tips and drenching you with showers of sticky pollen. Fortunately, the span of its gigantic wings and the narrowness of the plant's corolla conspire to prevent it from reaching deeper into the plant, and you are able to escape without sustaining further injury.

When you reach the bowl of the corolla once more, you lower yourself into the hollow stem and soon discover that it drops away very steeply. It is a vertical tube for most of its length, yet you are able to slow your rate of descent by grabbing hold of tiny tendrils which protrude from the lining of the stem wall. As you get nearer to its base, the stem wall becomes semi-transparent and slick with moisture. You press your face to this warm surface and you are able to discern other stems beyond. They look like the trunks of trees in a dense green forest. Then you look down to see that the stem of this plant is descending into darkness. The darkness begins at the point where the stem passes below ground level. You decide to stop at this point for you have no desire to explore the roots of this huge flower.

Carefully you examine the fabric of the semi-transparent stem. If you can force your way through this tough plant wall, you will be able to escape from your prison-like tube.

> If you possess a bladed weapon, or a bladed Special Item, turn to **332**.
>
> If you possess Kai-alchemy and wish to use it, turn to **57**.
>
> If you possess Magi-magic and wish to use it, turn to **279**.
>
> If you possess none of the above, or choose not to use them, turn to **4**.

145

You lose your grip and slip back into the water. As you make a second attempt to climb out, you feel the creature grab your legs. Swiftly he pulls you beneath the surface and drags you down towards the cellar floor, twenty feet below the surface. You are left in no doubt that this beast wants to drown you before it feasts on your flesh!

> If you possess Kai-alchemy, and have attained the Kai rank of Sun Thane, or higher, turn to **194**.
>
> If you do not possess this skill, or if you have yet to attain this level of Kai mastery, turn to **237**.

146

You step out from beneath the leaf under which

you have been hiding and focus on the distant vent. Carefully you recite the words of the Brotherhood spell *Levitation* that Guildmaster Banedon taught you many years ago, and moments later you feel yourself floating upwards through the air towards the apex of this gigantic cavern.

The spell frees you from the grip of gravity and enables you to soar towards the cavern's roof. However, you are unable to control the angle of your ascent and in order to steer yourself towards the vent, you must try to position yourself in one of the thermal currents which are rising from the canyon floor.

After some great effort you manage to locate a benign thermal which carries you slowly towards the distant vent. Unfortunately, you are not the only creature enjoying the hospitality of this rising current. You have soared close to a mile above the canyon when suddenly you attract the unwanted attention of a gigantic dragonfly. Anxious to defend yourself in case it should attack, you draw a weapon and wait with bated breath as it circles around your floating form.

Pick a number from the *Random Number Table*. If you possess Assimilance, add 1 to the number you have picked.

If your total is now 6 or less, turn to **75**.
If it is 7 or higher, turn to **244**.

147

Naar summons forth a shrieking horde of horrors from the smoky walls of his throne room. These hideous bat-winged creatures resemble deformed human brains that trail skeletal appendages. You retreat a few paces before them, in order to unsheathe your weapon, and then with your battle cry on your lips – 'For Sommerlund and the Kai!' – you launch yourself into their midst and fight like a demon.

Crypt Spawn horde:
COMBAT SKILL 50 ENDURANCE 36

If you win this combat, turn to **111**.

148

The once-grand doors of this hall no longer hang upon their hinges. They have been torn down and now lie twisted and rusted together, partially blocking the entrance. After checking to make sure that your adversary has not left any unwelcome surprises, you clamber over these ruined doors and begin a cautious exploration of the hall's gloomy interior.

The cavernous ground floor was long ago gutted by fire. All that remains of its contents now lie buried beneath blackened timbers and twisted iron beams. Metal chains hang in festoons from the buckled roof girders, dripping icicles of rust. They sway and squeal eerily in the wind, sending shivers coursing down your spine.

You detect nothing of interest in the debris and are about to abandon your search when suddenly you hear something unexpected – a dull thump. The sound came from below the ground. Drawing upon your Magnakai hunting skills, you peer through a hole in the ruined floor and detect something large and warm-blooded. It is moving away, towards the rear of the hall's cellar level.

If you wish to investigate your discovery further, turn to **168**.

If you choose to abandon your search and leave the hall, turn to **71**.

149

Caldar instructs one of his guards to escort you to the castle armoury, where you are encouraged to take whatever you need. From among the many racks of fine weapons and equipment, the following items catch your eye:

Broadsword
Sword
Axe
Warhammer
Short Sword
Mace
Spear
Arrows (6)

Quiver (counts as a Special Item if you choose this in addition to any quiver you may already possess)

Naptha Bomb (small explosive incendiary – counts as a Backpack Item)

If you choose to take any of the above items, make the appropriate adjustments to your *Action Chart*. You may then leave the armoury by turning to **260**.

150

Beyond the arch lies a steep ramp that descends to the floor of a circular chamber, the lowest level of the tower which soars into the stormy sky above. Runes of alien design run around the seamless glassy walls and the air is heavy with the sweet smell of decay. A large circular plinth stands in the centre of the chamber, its mirror-smooth surface a little under three feet from the floor. You take a step towards it and suddenly it is surrounded by a wall of fierce blue flames which shoot upwards from tiny vents in the floor around its base. As these flames gradually subside, you see four Kai Masters cowering upon the plinth. They are the four young Kai you thought had been left safely behind in the Old Necropolis of Tyso. They look petrified with fear, and when they see you they throw up their blistered, soot-blackened hands and plead for you to release them from their fiery prison.

Drawing upon your Magnakai Discipline of psi-screen, you detect that the image of the four Kai Masters is nothing but a cruel illusion. Then, in the very next instant, the ramp on which you are standing suddenly drops away from under your feet. You throw yourself to one side and crash down upon the floor of the chamber, rolling over as you strike the hard surface to lessen the shock of impact. As you stagger to your feet, you see the image of the four Kai being consumed by fire. It is a frightful sight, and as they scream their last, a wave of hostile psychic energy crashes into your mind.

If you possess Kai-screen, turn to **122**.
If you do not possess this Discipline, turn to **45**.

151

Wolf's Bane staggers backwards, clutching at his wounds with his free hand. You move forward, eager to finish him, but he parries your lunge and then, with a look of utter desperation in his soulless eyes, he glances up at the ceiling and shouts:

'Take him, Doom-blight! Take him now!'

Your blood freezes when you see a great gull-winged horror emerge from a hidden perch among the hall's shadowy rafters. It plunges towards you, a fiery sword held at arm's length ready to be driven through your heart.

> If you have ever encountered the Demoness Shamath in a previous *Lone Wolf* adventure, turn to **263**.
> If you have never encountered this creature, turn to **74**.

152

Frantically you shout the words of the Brotherhood spell *Halt Missile* and point at the onrushing arrow. The deadly shaft freezes in mid-flight, barely a few inches from the tip of your extended finger. Immediately you crouch down, and as the effects of the spell wear off, the shaft suddenly re-animates and whistles over your head to lodge itself in the tangle of vines that curtain the cave mouth.

Turn to **133**.

153

Icy fingers of fear run up and down your spine as

you brace yourself for the imminent impact of the approaching fire-bolt.

If you possess Kai-alchemy, and wish to use it, turn to **58**.

If you possess Magi-magic, and wish to use it, turn to **113**.

If you possess Assimilance, and have attained the rank of Sun Lord, (and you wish to use this Discipline), turn to **176**.

If you possess Grand Huntmastery, and have attained the rank of Sun Lord, (and you wish to use this Discipline), turn to **212**.

If you possess none of these skills, or do not yet possess the necessary level of Kai rank, (or if you choose not to use any Kai mastery), turn instead to **259**.

154

Dazed and trembling, you stagger to your feet and tentatively shake your head in an effort to clear your blurred vision. Close by your feet you see the outline of your weapon and you stoop to retrieve it. (If you were holding a normal weapon when you passed through the wall, you discover it has been destroyed by the blast: delete this weapon from your Weapons List. If the weapon you were holding was a Special Item, you discover that it has survived intact.)

As your vision returns you see that you have been hurled back into the chamber. Your fellow Kai, all of whom were knocked to the floor by the blast, are now struggling to get themselves back on their feet. Fortunately their physical injuries are minor; their innate Kai skills have spared them from serious injury. However, you sense that your inability to detect that the wall was an explosive illusion has severely shaken their confidence.

'Our prey is far more cunning than I feared,' you say, reproachfully, 'but we are Kai and we shall rise to the challenge. Our enemy possesses strong magic and he is capable of masking it well. Yet he chooses to use it to wound and weaken our party, not to kill us. Why this should be I do not know. But from now on we cannot entirely trust our senses to protect us. We must proceed with the utmost caution.'

Beyond where the illusory north wall once stood, you can now see a small antechamber which is wreathed in acrid blue smoke. Gradually this smoke dissipates to reveal a shallow plinth upon which lies a bronze urn. This heavy object rests on its side and a quantity of pale grey ash has spilled from its hinged lid. Cautiously you approach the urn and see that there is an inscription engraved on its side. From this ancient script you learn that the ashes are the last remains of Baroness Garrulen, the wife of Hul – third Baron of Tyso. Glinting half-buried in the ash, you notice a ring encrusted with crimson gemstones (if you wish to keep this Ruby Ring, record it on your *Action Chart* as a Special Item).

You are righting the urn on its plinth when you hear Steel Hand calling you. He has found something among the rubble which litters the floor at the rear of the antechamber.

Turn to **35**.

155

Before you can move to avoid the oncoming missile, it hits you in the chest and sends you crashing to the floor: lose 10 ENDURANCE points.

If you have survived this grievous wounding, turn to **56**.

156

With bated breath you watch as the warrior kicks the smouldering remains of the iron chest. He scans the warehouse, the visor of his helmet pulsing a dull crimson glow as he tries to locate where you are hiding. Unable to find you, he cradles his weapon and begins a systematic search of the building.

As he passes beneath the storage tank you seize the opportunity to launch a surprise attack. You leap onto his back and bring him crashing to the ground. However, you soon discover that he is an exceptionally strong opponent and your advantage of surprise is quickly lost. He draws his power from the armour he wears and you are hard pressed to maintain your hold on his neck as he wrestles to break free. Then another warrior appears at the rear of the building. He, too, is armed with a magical spear. He aims this weapon at you and a flash of light erupts from its tip.

Pick a number from the *Random Number Table*. If your current ENDURANCE points score is 12 or less, deduct 2 from the number you have picked.

If your total is now 0 or less, turn to **93**.
If it is 1 or more, turn to **63**.

157

The moment you destroy the mechanism, you feel a shuddering vibration run through the great iron portal. Slowly it grinds open to reveal an antechamber that is lit by a dozen flaming torches set around its glassy walls. The wind has now become so fierce that it is ripping your exposed flesh. Rather than remain outside in the storm a moment longer, you hurry through the open portal and seek shelter within.

Turn to **227**.

158

Despite your desperate action, you continue to sink further into this dry bog until the soil closes in over your head. You draw upon your Magnakai Discipline of Nexus to ease the pain in your aching lungs, but this simply prolongs your life for a further fifteen minutes before the lack of air and the crushing weight of the morass combine to overwhelm you.

Tragically, your life and your duel end here.

159

You insert the iron disc and the portal slides open to reveal an impressive sight. The chamber beyond is stacked to the ceiling with coils of wire and solid bars made of pure platinum. These items are worth a vast fortune on your home world of Magnamund. (If you wish to take a Platinum Ingot, record it on your *Action Chart*. Due to its weight, however, it occupies the same space as 2 Backpack Items.)

To leave this chamber and continue, turn to **330**.

160

The passage beyond the fissure twists and turns like an angry snake. Gradually this winding tunnel bears eastwards and descends by slope and stair into deeper levels of the catacombs. During your long trek you detect not a single trace of the impostor and, when eventually the tunnel comes to a dead end, you curse your ill luck. Reluctantly you decide to retrace your steps. It is only then that you sense a faint but lingering aura of evil close to the tunnel floor.

A closer inspection reveals a trapdoor set into the grimy flagstones. You pull this heavy hatch open and discover a circular chute and a ladder descending into darkness. Your heart misses a beat when you notice fresh tracks on the ladder's iron rungs; at last you have found the impostor's trail.

Cautiously you lead the descent into the chute, using your powers of infravision to scan for signs of movement in the damp darkness below. After several minutes you reach the bottom of the ladder where you discover a large vaulted chamber. Around its walls are positioned urns and grey stone caskets, each embellished with traces of gold. There is an unexpected air of opulence about this vault which prompts you to guess that it is a secret burial tomb.

If you have ever visited the Graveyard of the Ancients in a previous *Lone Wolf* adventure, turn to **182**.

If you have never visited this forbidden place, turn to **206**.

161

You approach the open door and pause momentarily to check that no glyphs or other traps have been placed here. The doorway is clear, and you can detect no lingering residues of magical energy that might betray the presence of illusions or shielding spells, so you rush through it and hurry down the flight of steps that descends beneath the ground.

The steps lead down to a tunnel that is dark and narrow. You sense danger ahead and, using your infravision, you detect Wolf's Bane standing at the far end of this passageway, some thirty yards distant. He is holding a long piece of rope which trails back along the tunnel towards you. You follow its course and see that it is attached to a wooden peg which holds secure the door to a cage set flush into the tunnel wall. You focus on the door and sense that the cage beyond is occupied by a large and ferocious carnivore. Wolf's Bane utters a chilling laugh as he whips the rope to dislodge the peg. But you focus on the peg and, using your Magnakai Discipline of Nexus, you cause it to jam. Your adversary curses you and casts aside the rope in frustration. Then he turns and disappears into a tunnel which meets this main passageway from the left.

Turn to **344**.

162

You race towards the swirling mouth of the Shadow Gate, but Naar is determined to launch one last desperate attempt to prevent you from

IX.   Before you can reach the gate, 2 of the rubbery-
limbed horrors hurl themselves upon you.

escaping. You are within ten paces of the gate when two of the rubbery-limbed horrors emerge from the smoky walls and hurl themselves upon you.

2 Cryopedeans: COMBAT SKILL 38 ENDURANCE 32

If you win this combat, turn to **350**.

163

Your defensive blow tears a hole in the creature's silvery wing. The wound is not fatal, but the damage to its wing is enough to render the hungry dragonfly incapable of ascending any higher. It emits a loud buzz of frustration which fades as it slowly spirals away towards a cluster of smaller creatures hovering near the centre of the gorge.

At length you reach the apex of the cavern and soar into the light-filled vent. Upon entering this vast aperture you are buffeted by crosswinds which sweep you precariously towards its rocky lip. Only your Kai Disciplines and your lightning-swift reactions save you from being crushed to death as you are blown towards its jagged, volcanic edge.

You survive the impact and are able to haul yourself out of the vent and climb safely onto a surface that you assume to be the roof of the cavern. Seeking shelter from the raging crosswinds, you squeeze yourself into a hollow in the porous rock from where you are able to take stock of your new surroundings. The sight makes you gasp, for it is a view that truly rivals the fertile wonders of the cavern below.

Turn to **239**.

164

Wary of the uncertain floor of this hall, you utter the words of the Brotherhood spell *Levitation* and feel yourself rising slowly to the ceiling. Using the gaps between the bricks in the arched roof, you pull yourself along the ceiling until you reach the far end of the hall. Fortunately, the door is unlocked and you are able to open it with your foot and lower yourself safely through its archway and into the hall beyond.

Turn to **62**.

165

You soon realize that the creature's iron collar and chain prevent it from reaching you so long as you keep your back pressed to the cavern wall. Mindful of this, you inch your way slowly towards the tunnel. However, you have progressed only a few yards when you feel the floor sloping away. The water is getting deeper.

If you possess Magi-magic, turn to **234**.
If you do not possess this Grand Master Discipline, turn to **25**.

166

Fortunately your attempt to evade this magical missile is successful. The onrushing bolt hits you only a glancing blow (lose 1 ENDURANCE point) before it slams into the wall of the shaft, showering you with harmless crimson sparks.

Make the necessary adjustment to your *Action Chart* and then continue by turning to **37**.

167

Once more you focus your advanced Kai senses on the gloomy entrance to the tomb. You can detect no living creature or imminent threat of ambush, yet the area around the doorway radiates traces of a malevolent magic that makes you deeply suspicious. However, you are mindful of the fact that the impostor has entered the catacombs by this door, and the longer you delay in tracking him, the more he increases his chances of successfully evading your hunting party.

If you wish to suppress your sense of unease and enter the tomb, turn to **72**.

If you choose to heed your senses and examine the entrance more closely, turn to **173**.

168

Carefully you lower yourself through the hole and drop silently to the floor of the cellar beneath. You remain crouched where you land, not daring to move a muscle until you have scoured the darkness for any potential threat to your life. You detect an area of warmth radiating from behind a stack of rotting timbers and slowly you inch towards it, your weapon drawn in readiness to strike.

You have moved to within a few yards of the timber pile and feel confident that you have tracked down your enemy.

'Come out, Wolf's Bane!' you shout, 'Don't hide from me like some cowardly dog!'

You sense movement and draw back your weapon in anticipation of your enemy's imminent attack. Then a loud, inhuman, blood-curdling howl issues from behind the pile of timber and in a terrifying moment your confidence is shattered. The enemy confronting you is not Wolf's Bane.

You glimpse the shadowy blur of a huge, black shape rising up from behind the timbers. Fangs gleam momentarily in the gloom as it opens its cavernous maw, and then, in the blink of an eye, it leaps over the pile and falls upon you.

Kataka: COMBAT SKILL 42 ENDURANCE 40

This creature is immune to all forms of psychic attack, except Kai-surge and Kai-blast.

If you win the combat, turn to **333**.

169

You hit the stinking water and dive beneath the surface. Your swift reactions save you from being hit and wounded, but when you rise from the stinking mire and claw the muck from your eyes, you are horrified to see the serpent's tail swishing back towards your chest.

Instinctively you throw yourself flat against the wall and its deadly barbed tail misses you by inches. As it sweeps past, you draw your weapon in readiness to strike out at it the moment it comes within range.

Ukara (chained): COMBAT SKILL 44 ENDURANCE 45

This serpent is immune to all forms of psychic attack, except Kai-surge.

If you win the combat, turn to **348**.

170

For what seems like an eternity, you plummet into the swirling heart of a supernatural vortex. Brilliant sparks and flashes of colour illuminate this funnel of darkness as items of furniture from the banquet hall explode and disintegrate, unable to withstand the extraordinary pressures generated by this cosmic whirlpool. You watch with shock and awe as the lifeless body of your adversary – Wolf's Bane – is transformed into a fiery meteor before your very eyes. Then, gradually, the spin of the vortex becomes less fierce and you feel the centrifugal pull on your body easing. Beams of light penetrate the darkness and you see Alyss glide into view. She appears to be reclining, as if casually resting upon a couch after a weary day's work, and her expression is mildly pensive. She looks as if to her this whole terrifying journey is nothing more than an irritating inconvenience.

At last the vortex slows to a standstill and you feel ground solidifying beneath your feet. But the darkness gives way to a swirling mist which dissolves to reveal a horrifying sight. A deep and morbid terror returns to twist its knife in your guts when you suddenly realize where you are. You have been summoned to the throne hall of Naar – the seat of power of the King of the Darkness – the inner sanctum of ultimate evil.

Turn to **331**.

171

Frantically you examine the portcullis, searching for some chink in its armour that you can exploit to your advantage. It is crudely constructed from tightly criss-crossing strands of iron and steel, bolted and riveted wherever the bars connect, yet despite its crude appearance you soon discover that it is very tough and secure. You will not be able to break through this portal.

If you possess Kai-alchemy, and have attained the rank of Sun Knight or higher, turn to **272**.

If you do not possess this Grand Master Discipline, turn to **55**.

172

You muster your skill and plunge your hand into the water, close to where the creature's head has surfaced. In an instant, the black water around its neck and body freezes over, trapping and crushing the beast within a solid block of ice.

Free now to continue your pursuit, you leave the frozen cellar-beast and climb the steps to emerge amongst the ruins of the city. There is no sign of Wolf's Bane, but when you hurry to where you saw him last, you discover a flight of steps leading down into a wide underground passage. His tracks can be seen clearly imbedded in the muddy floor of this tunnel.

The tunnel passes under a broad avenue and then surfaces in front of a grand two-storey building. This was once a busy warehouse that stored braided coils of fine copper cable. You avoid the main entrance in case your adversary is lying in ambush there, and enter instead by way of a flight of iron steps that leads to a second floor window. The moment you set foot inside the building you sense that Wolf's Bane is here. Warily you explore, your nerves stretched to breaking point as your eyes seek out detail in the darkness. You are approaching the west wing of this building when you suddenly catch sight of your opponent through a hole in the floor. He is sitting on his haunches behind a mound of wooden crates, busily eating a green-skinned fruit, and he is unaware that you are watching him.

If you possess Magi-magic, and have attained the rank of Grand Thane (and wish to use your skill), turn to **81**.

If you possess a Bow, and wish to use it, turn to **106**.

If you possess Kai-alchemy, and wish to use it, turn to **319**.

If you possess none of these skills, or have yet to reach the required level of Kai rank, or simply choose not to use them, turn instead to **20**.

173

Cautiously you inch your way nearer to the open tomb. Lying across the threshold is a slab of stone which stirs your curiosity. A closer inspection reveals an intricate design scratched upon its surface. It has been smeared with dirt and a magical spell of shielding has been placed upon it to disguise its true purpose. Yet you realize immediately what it is and you recoil from the slab, hurriedly retreating a dozen paces. It is a glyph of power: a magical booby trap that has been expertly camouflaged to keep it secret. If anyone or anything were to step upon or pass over this glyph, the energy contained within it would be released in one devastating instant.

You warn the others of what you have found and tell them to retreat with you to a safe distance. From the cover of a gravestone, several yards from the tomb, you instruct Star Lynx to pick up a rock and hurl it through the open doorway. He selects an apple-sized chunk of granite and lobs it accurately into the open tomb.

Pick a number from the *Random Number Table*.

If the number you have chosen is *1–4*, turn to **211**.

If it is *5–9*, turn to **53**.

174

The moment you enter the mouth of the skull-rock you are engulfed by a dense fog that is icy-cold and impenetrable to your sight and senses. The thunderous noise of the temple's destruction ends abruptly, as if a great door has suddenly been closed upon it. You strain your Kai skills to aid your pursuit of Wolf's Bane but to no avail; the ivory-white fog hides everything, swamping and distorting your sense of time and direction.

You keep moving, forcing yourself onwards, even though the surface beneath your feet has become viscous and uncertain. After what seems like an eternity spent wandering through this cloudy limbo, you gradually feel the ground hardening and sense that the impenetrable fog is beginning to dissipate. Patches of grey appear in the creamy whiteness. Then the fog dissolves completely and you find yourself standing in the middle of a rubble-strewn street, surrounded by the bleak and derelict remains of a decaying, alien city.

It is the dead of night and a fine drizzle falls from a storm-laden sky, dampening this dreary landscape. Everywhere you look you see the hollow shells of buildings. They are heaped with mounds of broken stone, twisted rusty iron, and shattered glass. There are no trees, no blades of grass, no animals here. Everything is cold, grey, and dead.

You examine the paved surface of the street and detect your enemy's footprints. They are fresh and they lead you to a small courtyard flanked by two buildings: a large municipal hall and a smaller two-storey dwelling. Wolf's Bane's tracks end in the middle of the wet courtyard and you sense that they have been deliberately erased. Despite your advanced hunting skills, you are unable to determine into which building your enemy has escaped.

If you wish to enter the municipal hall, turn to **148**.

If you wish to investigate the two-storey dwelling, turn to **267**.

175

The giant serpent resists your mental command to retreat, yet the strain of doing so leaves its body in a state of partial paralysis. Cautiously you advance, keeping a wary eye on its trembling form as you skirt around the serpent and inch your way towards the opposite tunnel. However, you have progressed only a few yards when you feel the floor sloping away beneath your feet. The water is getting deeper.

If you possess Magi-magic, turn to **234**.

If you do not possess this Grand Master Discipline, turn to **25**.

176

You use your Kai mastery to blur the outline of your body in the hope that the onrushing bolt of energy will miss its mark.

Pick a number from the *Random Number Table*. For every level of Kai rank you have attained above that of Grand Guardian, add 1 to the number you have picked.

If your total is now 4 or less, turn to **291**.

If it is 5 or higher, turn to **166**.

177

You pick up the ticking bomb and examine it carefully. Below the illuminated panel, which is counting down the seconds, you see four small windows which display a sequence of numbers. Beneath these windows are tiny buttons which, when pressed, change the numbers that are displayed. The third window in the sequence is blank and, when you concentrate upon it, your Kai senses reveal to you that by keying-in the missing number in the sequence you will prevent the bomb from exploding.

Study the following sequence of numbers carefully. When you think you know the solution, turn to the page number that is the same as your answer.

If you guess incorrectly, or if you cannot determine the missing number, turn instead to **269**.

178

Your psychic powers prove very effective: the giant insect obeys your command not to attack. Yet, before it flys away, it sprays the stamen with a misty vapour which causes the petals to close up.

Hurriedly you retreat along the stamen and narrowly avoid being crushed to death as the huge petals fold in on themselves. Your innate Kai Discipline of Animal Control has saved you from a confrontation with the giant insect, yet the creature has used its own innate abilities to thwart your chances of escaping from the plant this way. The vapour condenses and runs along the stamen, making it difficult for you to maintain your grip, and reluctantly you are forced to retreat all the way down to the bowl of the corolla, to where the hollow stem is now the only chance you have of getting out of this plant alive.

Turn to **103**.

179

Unfortunately you are detected by one of the grey-skinned creatures as you pass directly over their fluid-filled trough. It raises the alarm and frantically its ragged brothers scramble to unshoulder and load their bows.

If you possess Kai-alchemy, turn to **198**.
If you do not possess this Grand Master Discipline, turn to **231**.

180

Arrows splash into the mire, dangerously close. You sense that this volley was not aimed at you; it was let loose in the hope of hitting you by chance. Anxious to avoid a second volley, you increase your pace and sprint across the vault towards the exit tunnel.

Turn to **70**.

181

Your advanced psychic defences save you from sustaining severe damage to the fabric of your mind. However, the surprise assault on your mental defences has bought this castle guardian the precious few seconds he needs in which to advance upon you. As the pain in your head recedes, you see the armoured warrior striding towards you with his sword raised high, poised ready to deal you a mighty blow.

Meghanic: COMBAT SKILL 48 ENDURANCE 48

This being is immune to all forms of psychic attack, except Kai-surge and Kai-blast.

If you win the combat, turn to **338**.

182

Looking around the walls of this tomb brings back memories of the time that you ventured into the Graveyard of the Ancients. The shape of the urns which stand here are identical to those that you discovered by chance in the tombs beneath that forbidden burial ground. The recollection chills you, for clearly you recall that those urns contained deadly Crypt Spawn.

You focus your sixth sense on the urns that line this chamber and, to your relief, you detect no living creatures lurking within. You instruct the others to examine them with care and, to your surprise, they discover that some contain Laumspur leaves. They are spotted with age but they still possess their healing powers. (There are enough leaves here for three potions of Laumspur. Each potion counts as one Backpack Item and will restore 4 ENDURANCE points when swallowed immediately after combat.)

You are helping Blazer to tilt one of the urns when a sudden and unexpected noise at the far end of the chamber sets your pulse racing.

Turn to **80**.

183

Kekataag the Avenger is attired in battle armour that glimmers like slime-dulled gold. Beneath his helmet there is a hollow skull-face from which emerges a sickly stench that permeates even the foul air of this hall. The skulls and bones of humans bedeck his armoured hide and in his mighty hands he carries a great two-handed axe, its blade stained black with the blood of his countless victims.

This fearsome warrior holds you with his glowing eyes and you feel waves of powerful psychic energy buffet your mind. Your advanced Kai defences repel this attack, but you are left in no doubt that he is deeply jealous of your supposed defeat of Lone Wolf.

Turn to **255**.

184

You call upon your advanced mastery to mask the goodly aura that radiates from your body. Then, having mustered your Kai camouflage skills, you enter the vault and make your way stealthily towards the exit on the far side.

Pick a number from the *Random Number Table*. If you possess Assimilance and Grand Huntmastery, add 2 to the number you have picked.

If your total score is 5 or less, turn to **313**.
If it is 6 or higher, turn to **236**.

185

You race towards the hover-wagon and, as it sweeps by, you hurl yourself towards its open cargo bay. You hit the side of the vehicle with numbing force (lose 2 ENDURANCE points), but you manage to keep your grip and haul yourself aboard.

By the time the wagon reaches the windswept moat, you have concealed yourself in amongst it cargo of steel cylinders and bales of wire. You hear the distant clang of a bell and, from your hiding place, you are able to watch as the drawbridge extends from beneath the portal to span the deep chasm. Swiftly the wagon passes across the semi-transparent bridge and glides through the tower's open portal unchallenged.

Turn to **42**.

186

Your killing blow opens a gash across the giant insect's belly and brings the creature crashing down into the plant's corolla. Hurriedly you retreat along the stamen and narrowly avoid being crushed to death beneath its huge rainbow-coloured torso. You have triumphed in combat, yet the creature's death has thwarted your chances of escaping this way. Slippery ichor drips from its fatal wound and runs along the stamen, making it difficult for you to maintain your grip, and the bulk of its lifeless body now blocks any chance of your being able to escape upwards.

Reluctantly you are forced to retreat all the way down to the bowl of the corolla, to where the hollow stem is the only chance you now have of getting out of this sinister plant alive.

Turn to **103**.

187

᠆ concentrate your attention upon the cutting
᠆f your weapon and, using your advanced
᠆e tongues of magical flame to ignite along
᠆th. Then you vigorously attack the sticky

strands of the net and cleave through them with surprising ease. They shrivel at the touch of your fiery weapon and drop in smouldering heaps onto the floor of the tunnel. Within a matter of seconds you have cut a path through and are able to continue your pursuit.

Turn to **316**.

188

You approach the hut and crouch down beside its mud wall, close to its open door. Your senses detect no glyphs or other traps here, and there are no residues of magical energy that might betray the presence of illusions or shielding spells. However, your Kai senses do detect a strong aura of evil lingering at the rear of the hut, close to the water's edge.

You move around to the rear of this hovel and discover that the bank is deeply undercut where the soft earth has been eroded by the fast-flowing stream. Standing in a line in the shadow of the undercut are a dozen wooden cages, each containing a fleshless skeleton. A shiver runs down your spine as your Magnakai Discipline of Divination detects the lingering agonies of these luckless victims. They suffered cruelly at the hands of the natives of this settlement before death finally ended their torment. The shock of your discovery is unnerving: lose 1 ENDURANCE point.

You leave the stream and return to the front of the hut. Inside the open doorway you discover several fruits stacked in mounds on a mat of woven rushes. Somewhat to your surprise, your senses reveal that they are nutritious and safe to eat. (There are sufficient fruits here for 3 Meals.)

Wary of further delay, you approach the trench at the centre of the hut and descend a flight of steps that lead down to an underground tunnel. You can detect no traps, yet you have gone only a few yards along this narrow passageway when you hear the terrifying roar of a large cat. With an abruptness that takes your breath away, a huge tiger-like beast comes bounding from out of the darkness ahead. So sudden and unexpected is this creature's attack, that you only just have time in which to unsheathe a hand weapon as it hurls itself upon you.

Rahjaz: COMBAT SKILL 48 ENDURANCE 41

This creature is immune to all forms of psychic attack, except Kai-surge and Kai-blast.

If you win this combat, turn to **249**.

189

You ask Steel Hand to give you his rope and he obeys dutifully. You sling its coiled length around your shoulder and then you commence your climb. The rough, pitted wall offers many handholds and you progress swiftly to the ceiling where you are able to work your way quickly across to the middle of the chamber, directly above the fissure. Once you are in position, you fix one end of the rope to an exposed stone beam and cast the other end to your companions waiting below. One by one you watch them swing across the void and, when all have crossed safely, you untie the rope and make your way over to the far side to join them.

'Come, my lords,' you say, anxious to waste not a minute more, 'we must press on. We've a trail to find.'

Turn to **160**.

190

You rush to the nearest dragonfly pen and use your Magnakai Discipline of Animal Control to subdue its hostile occupant. Reluctantly the creature submits to your will and allows you to climb upon its back. It has no saddle, and so you are forced to grip its scaly back as best you can as it rapidly takes to the air. Fear is running ice-cold in your veins as you urge the creature towards the open portal in the roof, for you know that the bomb is set to explode at any moment.

Pick a number from the *Random Number Table*.

If the number you have picked is *0–3*, turn to **335**.
If it is *4–6*, turn to **278**.
If it is *7–9*, turn to **218**.

191

You emerge from the cave mouth, staying as low as you can and making the most of what little foliage there is in the clearing. You are so successful that you come to within twenty yards of your enemy's hiding place before he spots your approach.

The sudden realization that you are so close shocks your adversary to the core. You see his mouth drop open, revealing teeth that show white against the green of the jungle, then he regains his senses and rapidly disappears into the undergrowth. Determined that you are not going to allow him to get away so easily, you leap to your feet and give chase.

Turn to **90**.

192

The sudden shock of impact nearly knocks you off the back of your flying steed. Frantically you scramble to regain your seat and, as you pull yourself upright, you notice that the enemy is now more than a hundred feet below; the momentum of its attack has carried it deeper into the cavern.

Your mount seizes its slim advantage and climbs as fast as it can to get away from the larger dragonfly. The enemy circles about, as if preparing to pursue, then it emits a loud buzz and changes its course. You watch with relief as it spirals away towards a cluster of smaller dragonflies that are hovering near the centre of the gorge.

Several minutes elapse before your tireless mount reaches the apex of the cavern and soars into the light-filled vent. Upon entering this vast aperture you are buffeted by crosswinds which sweep you and your air-steed precariously close to its rocky lip. The shock of the unexpectedly violent wind causes your mount to circle around the lip and attempt to dive back into the cavern. Blind with fear, it no longer responds to your commands, forcing you to take drastic action to avoid being carried back into the gorge. As you swoop past a rocky outcrop, you leap from the creature's back and abandon yourself to the mercy of the crosswinds. Only your Kai mastery and your lightning-swift reactions save you from being crushed to death as you are blown towards the jagged, volcanic edge.

Miraculously, you survive the impact and are able to haul yourself out of the vent and climb safely onto a surface that, you assume, is the roof of the cavern. Seeking shelter from the raging crosswinds, you squeeze yourself into a hollow in the porous rock from where you are able to take stock of your new surroundings. The sight makes you gasp, for it is a view to rival the fertile wonders of the cavern below.

Turn to **239**.

193

You are within a dozen paces of the stairs when suddenly one of the grey-skinned creatures turns and sniffs the air; it has detected your scent. It scans the hall and the moment its ghoulish eyes focus on your body it raises the alarm. Frantically, its ragged brothers scramble to the stairs to deny you access to the balcony and archway above.

6 Avarosi: COMBAT SKILL 44 ENDURANCE 48

You cannot evade this combat; you must fight these foes to the finish.

If you win the fight, turn to **325**.

194

Mentally you recite the words of the spell *Breathe Water* and feel strength coursing through your limbs as the pain in your air-starved lungs melts

X.   One of the grey-skinned creatures sniffs the air – it has
detected your scent.

away. The creature is unaware of your ability to survive underwater and this gives you a strong advantage; it is slow to react to your initial attack.

Ekmakon: COMBAT SKILL 40 ENDURANCE 25

Ignore any ENDURANCE point losses you may sustain in the first two rounds of this combat.

If you win the fight, turn to **9**.

195

'Release him, my lord,' says Banedon. The Baron, caught off-guard by the sudden disappearance of the magical shield and the Guildmaster's unexpected request, takes a step backwards and reaches nervously for his sword.

'Have no fear,' says Banedon, staying the Baron's hand, 'for we have here the real Grand Master of the Kai.'

'How can you be so sure?' retorts Caldar. Banedon smiles and points to the amulet that you wear around your neck.

'Look there,' he says. 'No agent of Naar could tolerate the touch of that goodly artifact. Banish your doubts, my lord. This man is Lone Wolf.'

Turn to **88**.

196

You place an arrow to your bowstring and draw it taut to your lips. Expertly you gauge the distance to your target and then let your arrow fly. It arcs into the jungle and slams into the tree behind which your enemy is part-hidden, peppering his face with splinters of damp wood.

He curses you, his teeth showing white against the green of the jungle as he spits out fragments of tree bark. Then he springs from his hiding place and disappears into the undergrowth. Determined that you are not going to allow him to get away so easily, you dash out of the tunnel and give chase.

Turn to **90**.

197

Having been detected, you attempt a hasty escape and sprint as fast as you can towards the exit. As you run, a volley of bone arrows comes whistling down from the iron cauldron. One of the arrows grazes your left shoulder and gouges a furrow of skin from the back of your left thigh. You stifle a cry, but the intense pain that grips your injured limbs warns you at once that the tip of the arrow was tainted with poison.

Your innate healing skills counter the poison before it can do its deadly work, but your body's defences draw heavily on your reserves of strength and the curing process leaves you feeling weak and light-headed: lose 4 ENDURANCE points.

To continue, turn to **70**.

198

You extend your right arm and point your hand at the trough below. Then you utter the words of the Brotherhood spell *Lightning Hand* and a familiar tingle rushes along your arm to explode into life at the tip of your index finger. A bolt of blue fire arcs downwards to the oily surface and, with a deafening *wumph!*, it ignites the liquid to create a blazing fireball. Greedily, this guttering ball of flame consumes the creatures who are gathered around the lip of the trough, sparing none. The heat from the blast buffets you and singes your tunic and cloak, but your body survives unscathed.

On reaching the balcony you speak the words which negate the effects of the *Teleport* spell, and the moment your feet touch the ground you hurry into the archway beyond.

Use of the *Teleport* spell has cost you 4 ENDURANCE points. Remember to make the necessary adjustment to your *Action Chart*.

To continue, turn to **50**.

199

The first thing you see are the creature's eyes. Like two strips of molten sulphur, they radiate a cold, yellow light. Then you glimpse the outline of its angular shoulders, its square snout, and its gleaming steel forelegs. Oily drool hangs from an iron jaw which is set with jagged blades. As this shocking jaw widens, you hear the whir of metal cogs and gears.

You can be fearless in the face of foes of flesh and blood, but this steel wolf strikes terror in your heart. You turn and flee towards the distant door, praying that it will lead to a safe haven from this bloodless beast, but you reach it only to discover that it is locked. Frantically you search for a bolt or a keyhole but there are none. Then you locate two squares of opaque crimson gemstone set into the wall. The squares are like those you encountered at the entrance to the temple of Avaros, yet these differ in one important respect: they are separated by a small slot.

If you possess an Iron Disc, turn to **261**.
If you do not possess this Special Item, turn to **210**.

200

Fiery winds sear your face and body as you, and your adversary, tumble headlong towards the whirling white heart of the vortex. Motes of fire stream past on all sides and a roaring wind howls like a demon in your ears. You pass through a cloud of sparkling vapour which wraps threads of silver light around your limbs and torso. As you emerge from the cloud, this shimmering cocoon grows tighter and tighter until the pain becomes almost unbearable.

If you possess Grand Nexus, and have attained the rank of Grand Thane, turn to **229**.
If you do not possess this skill, or if you have yet to attain this level of Kai mastery, turn to **281**.

201

The seething horde of needle-fanged horrors attempt to surround and overwhelm you. They seem undaunted by the divine glow of your wondrous blade – a blade that can seal their doom.

Cryopedeans: COMBAT SKILL 45 ENDURANCE 40

If you win this combat, turn to **350**.

202

To your amazement, the portal begins to rise of its own accord. You wait until it has risen a few feet and you are sure that no enemy awaits you on the other side, then you duck under the heavy iron plate and hurry into the tunnel beyond. As you run, you hear the portal slamming shut behind you with a dull reverberating boom.

Turn to **115**.

203

This psychic assault has been one of the worst you have ever experienced. You have survived it, but your Kai senses warn you that your ordeal has not ended; it has only just begun. You force open your eyes and look with dread at the terrible threat that waits to confront you.

Turn to **300**.

204

You feel a searing wave of heat wash over your body as the fireball reaches its peak and then rapidly dies to form a spluttering flame which clings to the mouth of the fountain. None of the creatures have survived the conflagration and you are able to cross the hall and ascend the stairs to the balconied archway without meeting any resistance.

To continue, turn to **50**.

205

Guided by your Kai mastery, you successfully avoid the tumbling debris until you reach the base of the skull-rock. Here you are struck by a falling boulder which clips your left shoulder and leaves you sprawled on the floor: lose 4 ENDURANCE points.

Your arm may be injured but your spirit refuses to give up. Cradling your injured arm, you stagger to your feet and hurry through the misty opening. Barely seconds later there is a tremendous explosion and the entire temple ceiling caves in.

In addition to the ENDURANCE points loss, you soon discover that you have also lost 1 Backpack Item. Delete from your *Action Chart* the third item you have recorded on your list of Backpack Items.

To continue, turn to **174**.

206

Wary of danger, you focus your Kai sixth sense on the urns and caskets which line this chamber and, to your relief, detect no evil creatures lurking within. You instruct the others to examine them with care and, to your surprise, they discover that some contain Laumspur leaves. They are spotted with age but they still possess healing powers. (There are enough leaves here for three potions of Laumspur. Each potion counts as one Backpack Item and will restore 4 ENDURANCE points when swallowed immediately after combat.)

You are helping Blazer to tilt one of the urns when a sudden and unexpected noise at the far end of the chamber sets your pulse racing.

Turn to **80**.

207

You lower yourself through the hole and catch sight of Wolf's Bane running away. He is clutching at his injured leg as he weaves and swerves to avoid the debris which litters his escape route. You move to follow him, but your attention is momentarily distracted by something that has fallen from his tunic pocket. It is a small disc of bronze that is engraved with alien symbols. (You must keep this Bronze Disc. Record it on your *Action Chart* as a Special Item. You must discard one non-weapon Special Item in its favour if you already hold the maximum number permissible.)

You pocket the disc and give chase. Despite his wounded leg, your adversary is more familiar with this treacherous cityscape and he widens the gap between you. Soon you have lost sight of him completely. However, he cannot shake you off his trail, and you have no difficulty following his tracks as they leave the building and wend their way across a desolate wasteland beyond. You follow his footprints to a gutted building, several storeys high, which is adorned with strangely angular gargoyles. The inside of this crumbling edifice is completely empty and your adversary's trail passes through it to a rear exit. As you emerge on the far side, you catch your first breathtaking glimpse of this grim city's tallest structure.

It is a great tower of gleaming black stone which rises from the depths of a fathomless moat and soars to within a hundred feet of the stormy grey clouds. Its pitted surface bristles with metal discs and antennae, streaked with rust, yet there are few windows and you can see but one portal. Wolf's Bane is limping towards it. He approaches the deep trench that rings the tower's base and, as he halts at the edge, a semi-transparent drawbridge extends from beneath the portal. It resembles a flattened beam of solid, green-grey light. This beam bridges the moat and provides your enemy with a means to reach the open tower door.

Powerless to stop him, you can only stand and watch as he crosses the moat and disappears into the tower. At first glance this stronghold looks to be impregnable, but you have gained access to far tougher fortresses in the past and you do not allow your spirits to be dampened by the difficult task of finding a way into this one.

Turn to **308**.

208

Drawing upon your Animal Mastery, you will the giant snake to retreat towards the far wall of the cavern. Its hypnotic eyes widen and its huge body trembles as it struggles to resist your psychic command.

Pick a number from the *Random Number Table*. Add 1 to the number you have picked for every level of Kai mastery you have attained above the rank of Kai Grand Guardian.

If your total score is now 6 or less, turn to **175**.

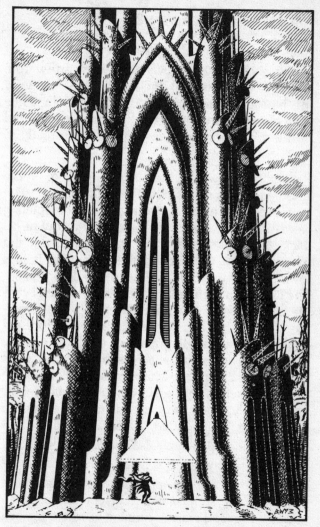

XI. Powerless to stop Wolf's Bane, you can only stand
and watch him disappear into the tower.

If it is 7 or more, turn to **32**.

209

You unshoulder your bow and draw an arrow from your quiver. As you fix the notch of the arrow to the bowstring, you cast the Old Kingdom battle spell *Flameshaft* upon its tip, keeping the last word of the spell upon your lips until you are ready to fire.

Patiently you watch the warrior kicking at the smouldering remains of the iron chest. The moment he turns away, you utter the completing word of the spell and let loose your arrow at his back. The tip of the arrow ignites in flight, the magical flame illuminating the gloom as it arcs towards your unwary target with deadly precision. The fiery point penetrates deep into the metal canister strapped to the warrior's back and, in a terrifying instant, he and his sorcerous weapon are engulfed by a crackling mass of electrical energy. He screams and staggers across the floor, his limbs and torso trailing blue-white snakes of light which earth themselves to the surrounding metal debris. Then, finally, the energy that is contained within the canister is expended. Released from his torment, he loses his balance and falls heavily to the floor.

You shoulder your bow and move to descend from the top of the storage tank, but you freeze when you see a second warrior running to where the first has fallen. As he passes beneath the tank, you leap onto his back and bring him crashing to the ground. To your shocked surprise you discover that he is an exceptionally strong opponent. He draws power from the armour he wears and he uses it to break your grip. In desperation you utter the words of the Old Kingdom spell *Energy Grasp* and use it to discharge a powerful pulse of energy into the fabric of his armour. The effect is devastating. His armour disintegrates, crushing him to death as it crumples and compresses his body.

Turn to **21**.

<h2 style="text-align:center">210</h2>

The rasping growl of the metal wolf is steadily getting louder. The sinister sound makes your palms slick with cold sweat as you feverishly examine the door and the locking mechanism set into the wall nearby.

The gemstone squares are sensitive devices which secure this door. By tapping upon each of them a correct number of times you will cause the lock to disengage and the door will open. You place your fingers lightly upon the squares and feel the tell-tale vibrations that are the key to deciphering their secret code. Aided by your Kai skills, you are able to determine that the first code is equal to the number of *named* Kirlundin islands north of Egen. The second code is equal to the number of villages to the east of Ragadorn.

In order to discover the exact numbers that will open the door, consult the map at the front of this book.

When you think you know the two-digit solution, turn to the entry that is the same number as your answer.

If you cannot decipher the codes, turn instead to **134**.

211

The moment the rock passes over the glyph there is a blinding flash of white light, followed almost instantly by the deafening crackle of exploding electrical energies. Splinters of stone ricochet from the gravestone behind which you and your fellow Kai have wisely taken cover, and the stench of scorched earth and ozone assails your nostrils.

Then, abruptly, the noise and light cease and the burial ground is shrouded once more in gloomy silence. You peer over the gravestone to see that the doorway is now clear of rubble, save for the slab upon which the glyph is inscribed. The destructive power of the glyph has been discharged, but only temporarily. Your senses warn you that it is recharging; you have but a few seconds in which to enter the tomb before the magical device is active once more.

'Quickly, my lords,' you say, as you spring to your feet and hurry towards the entrance, 'Follow me!'

Turn to **131**.

212

You call on your advanced Kai mastery to protect you from the effects of being struck by a massive electrical charge. However, the bolt that is now speeding towards your head is not a natural phenomenon – it is wholly magical in nature. The protection of your advanced Discipline may not be sufficient to save you from this crackling bolt of magical fire.

Pick a number from the *Random Number Table*. For every level of Kai rank you have attained above that of Grand Guardian, add 1 to the number you have picked.

If your total is now *3* or less, turn to **291**.
If it is *4* or higher, turn to **166**.

213

You hear the pot splash into the mire and the sound makes you spin around and reach for your weapon. The two angry reptilians clamber out of the pot and come rushing at you with jagged bone swords clutched tightly in their hands. They hiss and howl as simultaneously they launch themselves upon you.

2 Knoarcs: COMBAT SKILL 48 ENDURANCE 41

These beings are immune to all forms of psychic attack, except Kai-surge and Kai-blast.

If you win this combat, turn to **129**.

214

You retreat along the stamen as fast as you can, yet the sticky pollen conspires to slow you down. Then there is a sudden rush of air and you are forced to flatten yourself behind a gluey pollen cluster as the insect's lance-like proboscis comes hurtling towards your back.

Pick a number from the *Random Number Table*. If you possess the Disciplines of Grand Pathsmanship

XII. The angry Knoarcs come rushing at you, tightly
clutching jagged bone swords.

and Assimilance, add 2 to the number you have picked.

If your total score is now *0–4*, turn to **295**.
If it is 5 or higher, turn to **22**.

215

From the cover of the leafy undergrowth you observe the primitive settlement for several minutes. During this vigil, you are bitten on the wrist by a small, ugly-looking spider which you crush immediately under your heel. The spider's bite is poisonous, but you are saved from a long and painful death by your innate Kai healing powers which eradicate the venom from your blood: lose 3 ENDURANCE points.

As time ticks by you become increasingly restless. You can detect no signs of life around the settlement and you are haunted by the fear that you may have allowed your adversary's trail to go cold. Prompted by this anxiety, you move closer to the settlement under cover of the thick jungle foliage. The line of deserted mud huts look innocuous, but the words of the voice of Naar still linger in your memory. This humid jungle realm lies within his domain; it is therefore reasonable to expect that any inhabitants of this place will be wholly devoted to the cause of Evil.

You reach the edge of the undergrowth and pause to assess potential threats. The huts are semi-derelict, all bearing some signs of neglect and decay. The nearest one is a clay-tiled hovel that, like the others, appears to be empty. But when you focus upon its open doorway you see that a trench has been cut into its earth floor. You magnify your vision and at once you detect steps in the wall of this excavation, leading underground.

If you wish to enter the hut and investigate where these steps lead to, turn to **306**.

If you choose instead to check the hut for traps, turn to **27**.

216

In response to your prayer, you feel a warm and glowing sensation deep within your chest. This feeling grows and then pulses through your body and your mind, leaving you physically and mentally refreshed and alert: restore 8 ENDURANCE points.

Confident that the divine Gods of Good are watching over you in your moment of truth, you throw open the doors and stride boldly into the hall beyond.

Turn to **240**.

217

You unsheathe your weapon and dive aside to avoid the Bangrol as it swoops out of the chimney and attempts to claw you with its razor-sharp talons.

Bangrol: COMBAT SKILL 34 ENDURANCE 30

If you win this combat in 3 rounds or less, turn to **142**.

If the combat goes to a fourth round, do not continue the fight. Instead, turn immediately to **19**.

218

You escape through the steel roof of the tower and catch a fleeting glimpse of the rainswept city far below. Suddenly there is a tremendous flash as the bomb explodes and a debris-laden shockwave hits you from behind, flattening you against the dragonfly's crusty neck: lost 3 ENDURANCE points.

Your winged mount is hit by twisted metal from the blast which tears open its vulnerable belly. You feel it shudder, and then, in a terrifying instant, it ceases to beat its gossamer wings. Moments later you find yourself clinging desperately to its back as it plummets towards the ruins of the alien city.

If you possess Deliverance, and have attained the rank of Sun Knight, turn to **76**.

If you do not possess this skill, or if you have yet to attain this level of Kai mastery, turn to **226**.

219

You recite the words of the Old Kingdom battle spell *Shield* and circle your arm in a wide arc before you. The reptilians cackle with glee as they finish reloading their bows, and together they lean over the lip of the pot and take aim at your seemingly unprotected body. Simultaneously they let fire, sending a stream of arrows whistling towards your chest, but none of them find their mark. The bone shafts shatter to pieces as they smash into your invisible shield.

Your thwarted enemies curse you vilely as they fumble to reload once more. It will take them less than a minute to achieve this task and so, mindful of the impending danger, you turn and hurriedly examine the sealed portal for a lever or some other means to make it rise.

Turn to **18**.

220

You can feel a warm breeze wafting along this new hallway and you sense that it comes from a stairwell at its far end. When you investigate it, you rediscover Wolf's Bane's footprints on the stone steps. You cast your hands over them and detect that this is not a false trail: your enemy passed this way sometime within the last hour.

Slowly you ascend the stairs and arrive at the arched entrance to a large, vaulted stone chamber. Gathered around a fountain set into its north wall are a group of six grey-skinned humanoids. They are busy drinking a clear, oily fluid that pours from the fountain's spout into a semi-circular trough. All are barefoot and clad in rags, and they are each armed with a spear and a bow. The only exit from this chamber appears to be an archway set high in the north wall. There is a balcony in front of it that can only be reached by two flights of stairs which rise up on either side of the fountain.

Quietly you observe the creatures slaking their thirsts, and you try to formulate a way in which you can get past them and reach the balconied exit in the north wall.

If you possess a Bow, and the Discipline of Magimagic, and have attained the rank of Kai Grand Guardian, turn to **138**.

If you possess Kai-alchemy and have attained

the rank of Grand Crown (and wish to use it), turn to **26**.

If you do not possess these skills, or a Bow, or if you have yet to attain the required levels of Kai mastery, turn to **121**.

221

The shock of impact sends you tumbling helplessly into the gorge. You fall several hundred feet before you finally stop spinning, yet before you can unscramble your senses, you are struck from behind by the predatory dragonfly. White hot pain shoots through your body as you are impaled upon the tip of the creature's proboscis. You struggle to get free but your strength quickly deserts you. Mercifully, you are spared further agonies when you slip into unconsciousness – the prelude to a sleep from which you never awaken.

Sadly, your life and your quest end here.

222

You have leapt and scrambled your way to the base of the skull-rock, when suddenly a starburst of pain explodes in your head and the taste of blood fills your mouth. You fall face-first to the ground, breaking your nose on impact, but you are numb to the pain; a falling boulder has already snapped your neck in two.

Tragically, your life and your duel come to an end here.

223

The blast sends you tumbling backwards into the chamber. The instant you come to rest, you roll over onto your hands and knees and try to scramble back onto your feet. But before you can do so, something heavy strikes your side and knocks you down, pinning your legs to the ground. You reach out to pull yourself free and discover that the heavy object is Black Hawk. Dazed and trembling but otherwise uninjured, you drunkenly help each other to stand.

Once you are upright, you look around and see that the others have all been knocked flat by the blast. They, too, are now struggling to pull themselves to their feet. Fortunately their innate Kai skills appear to have spared them from serious injury. However, you sense that your inability to detect that the wall was an explosive illusion has shaken their confidence.

'Our prey is far more cunning than I feared,' you say, reproachfully, 'but we are Kai and we shall rise to the challenge. Our enemy possesses strong magic and he is capable of masking it well. Yet he chooses to use it to wound and weaken our party, not to kill us. Why this should be I do not know. But from now on we cannot entirely trust our senses to protect us. We must proceed with the utmost caution.'

Turn to **345**.

224

You lower yourself through the hole in the floor and quickly give chase. Wolf's Bane sprints through the ruined building, leaping obstacles with a cat-like grace that rivals your own legendary agility. He is more familiar with this treacherous cityscape and, despite your best efforts, he soon widens the gap between you until you lose sight of him completely. Yet he cannot shake you off his trail, and you have no difficulty following his tracks as they leave the building and wend their way across the desolate wasteland beyond. You follow his footprints to a gutted building, several storeys high, which is adorned with strangely angular gargoyles. The inside of this crumbling edifice is completely empty and your adversary's trail passes through it to a rear exit. As you emerge on the far side, you catch your first breathtaking glimpse of this grim city's tallest structure.

It is a great tower of gleaming black stone which rises from the depths of a fathomless moat and soars to within a hundred feet of the stormy grey clouds. Its pitted surface bristles with metal discs and antennae, streaked with rust, yet there are few windows and you can see but one portal. Wolf's

Bane is running towards it. He approaches the deep trench that rings the tower's base and, as he halts at the edge, a semi-transparent drawbridge extends from beneath the portal. It resembles a flattened beam of solid, green-grey light. This beam bridges the moat and provides your enemy with a means to reach the open tower door.

Powerless to stop him, you can only stand and watch as he crosses the moat and disappears into the tower. At first glance this stronghold looks to be impregnable, but you have gained access to far tougher fortresses in the past and you do not allow your spirits to be dampened by the difficult task of finding a way into this one.

Turn to **308**.

225

Using your psychic and pathsmanship skills, you focus your attention on the iron pot and determine that the two creatures lurking inside are armed with a variety of weapons. Your acute senses detect the presence of bone, oiled twine and bronze, as well as some volatile chemicals which you cannot identify. Also, you sense that they possess very sensitive hearing and are receptive to goodly auras. There is a very great risk that if you attempt to cross the vault undetected, relying solely on your advanced camouflage skills, these ambushers would be able to detect you using their own innate abilities.

If you possess Kai-screen, and have attained the rank of Kai Grand Crown, turn to **184**.
If you do not possess this skill, or if you have yet to attain this level of Kai mastery, turn to **105**.

226

You draw upon your Magnakai Disciplines of curing and animal control in a desperate attempt to revive your unconscious mount before it is too late.

Pick a number from the *Random Number Table*. If your current ENDURANCE points score is 20 or higher, add 1 to the number you have picked. If it is 10 or lower, deduct 1.

If your total score is *2* or less, turn to **89**.
If it is *3* or higher, turn to **346**.

227

The iron portal grinds to a close behind your back, shutting out the storm so completely that the roar of the wind instantly disappears. The abrupt silence and lower air pressure within this entry chamber makes your ears pop painfully. You lower the hood of your cloak and carefully wipe the sand from your eyes before taking your first tentative steps across the antechamber's polished glass floor.

You pass through a triangular arch and down a ramp that leads to an echoing hallway. The floor and walls of this broad hall are fashioned from a black glassy mineral that is veined with fluorescent greens and sickly purples. You sense strong pulses of psychic power radiating from an open arch at the far side of the hall and your skin prickles with a presentiment of danger. You unsheathe your weapon and move towards the arch with the utmost caution; you are expecting the unexpected.

Turn to **150**.

228

It takes you nearly half an hour to cleave a path through these magical strands, and the effort leaves you tired and aching with fatigue.

Pick a number from the *Random Number Table*. If the number you have picked is 0–4, reduce your ENDURANCE score by 1 point. If the number you have picked is 5–9, reduce your ENDURANCE score by 2 points.

To continue, turn to **316**.

229

Rapidly the pain melts away as your advanced Kai mastery sheathes and protects you from the crushing grip of the vortex. The strands of light unravel themselves and dissolve as you plummet ever nearer to the blazing white heart of this cosmic whirlpool. Then, at the moment you plunge into its core, your senses are obliterated and you are engulfed by total darkness.

From out of the depths of this cold dark universe there appears a pinpoint of light. You feel yourself being drawn inexorably towards it and, although you struggle to resist, you cannot tear yourself free from its irresistible pull. You feel yourself accelerating towards it until the speck becomes as large as a glowing sun. Then, with an abruptness that leaves you gasping, there is a flash of blue-white light and you find yourself lying spread-eagled upon a bed of moist green foliage.

Turn to **49**.

230

You leap from the rent in the plant wall and land safely on a mound of soft black earth. As you struggle to your feet, you notice that this rich soil forms a narrow clearing between the base of the plant and the stems of many others, all of a similar species. Their colossal stalks soar into a dimly amber sky where gigantic flowering heads bend and sway in a humid breeze. Staring at this awe-inspiring canopy, hundreds of feet above, makes you feel incredibly small and vulnerable – like a tiny insect. This feeling is made worse when suddenly a huge, horse-sized beetle comes careering through the plant stems. Instinct and quick thinking save your skin. Instantly you freeze and the shiny black monstrosity ignores you and continues its chaotic rampage through this forest of gigantic plants.

It is several moments before your pulse slows and

your senses detect a distant source of energy, somewhere away to the north. You cannot discern its nature or purpose but you feel compelled to investigate. Guided by your tracking skills, you trek through this extraordinary forest for nearly an hour before arriving at a huge clearing where, from the cover of a huge fallen leaf, you gaze upon a spectacular sight.

Turn to **334**.

231

You are rapidly approaching the safety of the balcony, yet two of the ghoulish creatures manage to aim and fire their bows at you before you disappear out of their field of fire.

Pick a number from the *Random Number Table*. If you possess the Discipline of Assimilance, add 3 to the number you have picked.

If your total score is now 2 or less, turn to **126**.
If it is 3 or higher, turn to **54**.

232

You throw yourself flat to the ground in a desperate attempt to avoid being hit by this deadly missile.

Pick a number from the *Random Number Table*. If you possess the Discipline of Grand Huntmastery, add 3 to the number you have picked.

If your total score is now 0, turn to **8**.
If it is 1–6, turn to **15**.
If it is 7 or higher, turn to **86**.

233

You cast the Brotherhood spell *Counterspell* at the sticky strands, and watch as they sag and smoulder. Your magic has weakened the fabric of this net, but it has not completely removed it. You are forced to draw a weapon and slash your way through the remaining strands in order to be able to continue along this tunnel. (The fatigue of overcoming this obstacle costs you 1 ENDURANCE point.)

Turn to **316**.

234

You recall the verses of the Old Kingdom spell *Hold Enemy* and as you whisper these arcane words, you focus upon the eyes of the chained serpent. Instantly, the creature ceases to thrash the water and falls silent and still, enabling you to wade across the deep channel which bisects this cavern.

Turn to **342**.

235

The tunnel zigzags to the left and right for several hundred yards before it widens at the entrance to a long, low-ceilinged hall. The slabs of stone which have so far paved the tunnel end abruptly at the entrance to this chamber. The floor here appears to be made of a gritty brown soil that gives off a pungent, earthy aroma. You scan its surface but you can see no tracks – it looks perfectly smooth.

If you possess Kai-alchemy, turn to **164**.
If you do not possess this Grand Master Discipline, turn to **48**.

236

You are within a few yards of the exit when suddenly you hear gleeful, rasping voices. You have been detected! Your immediate reaction is to bolt for the tunnel and, as you run, arrows whistle down to splash into the mire all around your feet. Anxious to avoid risking being hit by a second volley, you increase your pace as you approach the mouth of the tunnel.

Turn to **70**.

237

You feel the strength ebbing from your limbs as the pain in your air-starved lungs begins to worsen. You are near to the bottom of the flooded cellar when you manage to unsheathe your weapon and strike out at your rubbery foe.

Ekmakon: COMBAT SKILL 40 ENDURANCE 25

Reduce your COMBAT SKILL by five for the duration of this fight, due to your lack of oxygen.

If you win the combat, turn to **9**.

238

The Baron escorts you and Banedon through the echoing corridors of his castle, past watchful ranks of court guards and Border Rangers, to a hall which is lavishly furnished with Durenese oak and rare silken tapestries. Awaiting you there are a group of young men attired in hooded grey cloaks and close-fitting tunics. You recognize them immediately for they are four of your most promising students – Kai Masters Black Hawk, Star Lynx, Blazer and Steel Hand.

'Praise Ishir you've returned to us, Grand Master!' says Black Hawk, laying his right hand across his chest in a formal Kai salute. His companions breathe an audible sigh of relief as they, too, salute you and bow in deference to your rank.

'Stand easy, my lords,' you say, smiling as you motion them to relax. 'It warms my heart and gives me strength to be with you again.'

'We have heard the Guildmaster's account,' says red-haired Blazer, 'and we await your orders, my lord. Upon your command we will find the impostor and avenge the honour of the Kai.'

You are about to give your answer when a court herald announces the unexpected arrival of Lord Foilan, Reeve-lieutenant of Tyso, the man charged with keeping law and order in the city. Upon entering the hall he is momentarily taken aback by the sight of you standing at the Baron's side.

'Calm yourself, Foilan,' says Baron Medar, 'this is the true Lone Wolf, not the impostor who stalks our land. What news have you?'

'Sire . . . the Kai impostor has been sighted within the hour by rangers in the city's North Quarter. They tried to take him captive but he slew two and wounded three of their number before escaping into the old necropolis. The city watch now have both entrances to the necropolis secure – he will not be permitted to escape.'

'Very good, my lord,' retorts the Baron, 'so we have him cornered.'

XIII.   Awaiting you in the hall are four of your most
promising students: Black Hawk, Star Lynx, Blazer and
Steel Hand.

'If he's gone to ground in the old necropolis,' says Banedon, 'he'll be hard to track down. The catacombs of that ancient burial field are vast. It could take months to search them all.'

'Never fear,' you say confidently. 'With the help of my able young Kai Masters I shall track and trap this impostor before dawn.'

'Aye, my lord,' pipes Star Lynx, elated by the thought of the hunt, 'we'll flush this cur from his hole before sunrise and bring him to justice.'

Guided by Lord Foilan, you take your leave of Banedon and Baron Medar and depart from the castle on horseback, accompanied by your eager Kai. During your ride through the twisting, lantern-lit streets of Tyso, you learn from Foilan that there are only two ways in and out of the city's old necropolis: by its South Gate or by its Western Arch.

'The impostor fled into the burial ground by the South Gate, my lord,' says Foilan, 'but that was more'n an hour ago. He'll be deep un'erground by now.'

If you wish to ask Foilan to lead you to the South Gate of the necropolis, turn to **337**.

If you choose to ask that he take you to the Western Arch instead, turn to **323**.

239

Before your disbelieving eyes there spreads a vast volcanic landscape, punctuated by mountainous dunes of blue-grey sand and columns of towering rock. The amber sky is mottled and banded, like the eye of an angry tiger, and within its fathomless reaches you count twelve multi-coloured moons. These glowing spheres cast their light upon the burnt and crusty soil, lending it a ghostly aspect. Thick clouds, black and turgid, swollen with humid vapours, rear up like shadowy castles upon the far horizon. You can feel coarse grains of sand in the stinging crosswinds and your senses warn that a storm is fast approaching.

Seeking safer shelter from the coming storm, you get to your feet and cast your eyes across this warm yet unwelcoming land. Away to your right, lying less than a mile distant within a shallow basin of age-worn rock, you see a monstrous temple crafted from opaque black glass. Spikes of crystal embellish its many tiers and atop its highest level there stands a tower, tall and sleek.

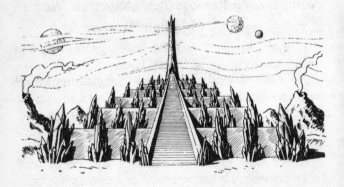

A square of yellow light marks an open portal at the tower's base. You glimpse something standing in the doorway and, when you magnify your vision, you see that it is a cloaked warrior silhouetted against the portal's fiery glow. Your pulse quickens the instant you recognize the warrior. It is your accursed adversary – Wolf's Bane.

The compelling urge to move northwards, that you felt shortly after you broke free from the plant stem, returns to haunt your senses. You feel drawn towards the temple as if you are being summoned by a force beyond this world. Your sixth senses scream danger, and every fibre of your being knows it should resist, but you suppress these natural instincts and set off towards the temple. This towering edifice holds many dangers, of that you are in no doubt, yet bravely you resolve to confront and overcome them. Only by doing so can you hope to triumph over your enemy and find a way back to your home world of Magnamund.

During your difficult trek to the temple, unless you possess the Discipline of Grand Huntmastery you must eat a Meal or lose 3 ENDURANCE points.

To continue, turn to **251**.

240

The doors swing open onto a gallery which encircles three sides of a large banquet hall. Below, through the wooden spindles of the gallery's parapet rail, you can see the hall itself. Tapestries drape the walls and a blazing fire crackles in a great stone fireplace that occupies much of the north wall. Your adversary is sitting alone in a throne-like chair at the head of a long banqueting table. A plain, oblong-shaped wooden case lies closed on the table before him.

'Welcome, Lone Wolf – so glad you could join me,' he says, his voice oozing sarcasm as he gets to his feet and tilts his head condescendingly towards the gallery. You see his right hand move below the edge of the table and, moments later, you hear the double doors swing shut and lock behind you. Anxiously you cast your eyes around the hall, searching out his hidden accomplices.

'We're alone,' snaps Wolf's Bane. He raises a hand and beckons you to descend the gallery stairs to the hall below. 'The time has come, Lone Wolf. Our jaunt across Avaros has been leading to this moment of truth.'

Wolf's Bane reaches out to the slim case that is laid on the table before him and he flips open its lid. Inside you see two thin-bladed duelling rapiers couched on a velvet liner.

'We two are as equally matched as these fine blades,' he says, in a voice as syrupy as rancid molasses. 'Come, Lone Wolf. I challenge you to duel honourably. Come and choose your weapon and let fate decide who of us will triumph this day.'

You magnify your vision and scrutinize the open case. Your senses confirm that these swords are finely crafted blades. They are not booby-trapped, nor are they magically cursed in any way.

If you choose to accept Wolf Bane's challenge to a duel to the death using these swords, turn to **304**.

If you choose to decline his challenge, turn to **85**.

241

Your psychic command weakens the Bangrol's

XIV. 'We're alone,' snaps Wolf's Bane. 'The time has
come, Lone Wolf.'

resolve, but it is already too late to turn aside its savage attack. This razor-clawed bird is set on a collision course with your face!

Bangrol: COMBAT SKILL 34 ENDURANCE 30

If you win this combat in two rounds or less, turn to **142**.

If the combat goes to a third round, do not continue the fight. Instead, turn immediately to **19**.

242

This lock looks similar to that which operates the door to the temple of Avaros, yet there is one important difference. The mechanism of this lock is genuinely protected by a powerful spell, shielded also by magic to prevent its detection. Your unsuccessful attempt to open the portal triggers this spell and causes a massive bolt of electrical energy to be discharged through your fingers, along your outstretched arm, and deep into your body.

A blinding flash of light obliterates your vision and an agonising pain explodes in your chest. The pain quickly fades, but it is replaced by a terrifying numbness. You feel weightless, as if you are falling through deep space. Briefly you try to resist this sensation but it is no use. You are falling into a sleep from which you will never awaken.

Sadly, your life and your duel against Wolf's Bane end here.

243

This exit leads to an echoing tunnel constructed from sheeted steel. Its walls and ceiling are lined with iron pipes and braided copper cables for most of its length. You follow this passage for several hundred yards before arriving at another which crosses it from left to right.

> If you possess Telegnosis, and have attained the rank of Grand Thane, turn to **73**.
> If you do not possess this skill, or if you have yet to attain this level of Kai mastery, turn to **347**.

244

The huge dragonfly swoops down like a hunting hawk and attempts to skewer you upon the sharp tip of its spear-like proboscis. You wait until the very last moment before twisting aside to avoid its lunge and, as it streaks past, you deal it a back-handed blow which tears a hole in its silvery wing. The wound is not fatal, but the damage to its wing is enough to render the hungry creature incapable of ascending any higher. It emits a loud buzz of frustration which fades as it slowly spirals away towards a cluster of smaller dragonflies hovering near the centre of the gorge.

At length you reach the apex of the cavern and soar into the light-filled vent. Upon entering this vast aperture you are buffeted by crosswinds which sweep you precariously towards its rocky lip. Only your Kai mastery and your lightning-swift reactions save you from being crushed to death as you are blown towards its jagged, volcanic edge.

You survive the impact and are able to haul yourself out of the vent and climb safely onto a surface that you assume to be the roof of the cavern. Seeking shelter from the raging crosswinds, you squeeze yourself into a hollow in the porous rock from where you are able to take stock of your new surroundings. The sight makes you gasp, for it is a view that truly rivals the fertile wonders of the cavern below.

Turn to **239**.

245

Your Kai camouflage skills keep you hidden from the unwanted attentions of the creatures below, and you reach the balcony without being seen. Once you are here, you whisper the words which negate the effects of the spell and then you hurry into the archway.

Use of the *Teleport* spell costs you 4 ENDURANCE points. Remember to make the necessary adjustment to your *Action Chart*.

To continue, turn to **50**.

246

You use your advanced mastery to find your enemy's tracks, and then you clear a path through the dense undergrowth which covers them. You sense that he has used magic to assist his escape, for the foliage here is entangled far tighter than in neighbouring areas of this jungle. Your advanced Discipline flattens the undergrowth as you advance, as if you were being preceded by some invisible battering ram. So effective is your skill that you gain ground on your fleeing enemy.

As you pass through a copse of toa trees, you hear the sound of running water away to your left. The tracks turn in this direction and you follow them all the way to the banks of a fast-flowing watercourse. Less than fifty yards downstream there is a primitive settlement of huts that form an untidy line along the banks of the stream. You catch sight of Wolf's Bane as he runs into this settlement and hides in the nearest hut – a mud-walled hovel with a clay tile roof.

If you wish to stay in the jungle and observe the settlement, turn to **339**.

If you choose to continue your pursuit, you can approach the settlement under cover of the jungle, by turning to **285**.

247

Steel Hand pulls a rope from his backpack and volunteers to climb the rough-hewn chamber wall. The ceiling above is criss-crossed with buttresses and he is confident that he can affix his rope securely to one of them, thereby enabling your party to swing across the gaping fissure and reach the tunnel on the far side.

If you decide to approve Steel Hand's suggestion, turn to **119**.

If you prefer instead to fix the rope yourself, turn to **189**.

248

You leap aside to avoid the missile, yet it alters course in mid-air and clips your shoulder as you fall to the frost-encrusted floor: lose 2 ENDURANCE points. Quickly you scramble to your feet and look to see your opponent escaping up the darkened staircase. Calling upon your innate healing skills, you staunch the blood that is trickling freely from your wounded shoulder and hurry towards the stairs in pursuit of your hated foe.

Turn to **29**.

249

Your killing blow fells this feline horror, bringing it crashing nose-first to the dirt floor. The body of the beast almost blocks the passageway, forcing you to clamber over it in order to reach the other side. You are struggling across its still-warm carcass when you notice a thick leather collar buckled around its throat. Affixed to the buckle is a curious Black Clasp (if you wish to take this clasp, record it on your *Action Chart* as a Special Item which you carry in the pocket of your tunic).

To continue, turn to **120**.

250

Before you stands a great tower of gleaming black stone which rises from the depths of a fathomless moat and soars to within a hundred feet of the stormy grey clouds. Its pitted surface bristles with metal discs and antennae, streaked with rust, yet there are few windows and you can see but one portal.

You magnify your vision and note that your adversary's tracks lead to a traffic-worn area on this side of the moat, directly opposite the portal. You watch this area for several minutes, and then you see two armour-clad warriors emerge from the ruins and approach it. Suddenly a semi-transparent drawbridge extends from beneath the portal. It resembles a flattened beam of solid, green-grey light, and this beam bridges the moat and provides the two warriors with the means to reach the open tower door.

You scan the great tower with your senses and you feel sure that your opponent is lurking somewhere within. Powerless to reach him, you can only stand and watch the two warriors as they cross the moat and disappear into the portal, which slides shut behind them. At first glance this stronghold looks to be impregnable, but you have gained access to far tougher fortresses in the past and you refuse to allow your spirits to be dampened by the daunting task of finding a way into this one.

Turn to **308**.

251

By the time you reach the base of the temple, the storm is howling like a vengeful demon in your ears. Stinging blasts of hot, sand-laden wind whip your face mercilessly and you are forced to lean almost horizontally into the storm to maintain your balance. The storm is increasing in ferocity by the minute. You are sorely aware that you must find cover within an hour at most or you will perish in this hellish blizzard.

An empty parapeted stairway ascends from the temple's lowermost tier to the portal of its crowning tower. The parapet offers you protection from the wind and you climb the many steps bent over, almost on your hands and knees, in order to stay out of the abrasive storm. Before you ascend the last tier, you check to make sure that your adversary is not lying in ambush. The portal is now closed and you can sense no living creature nearby, yet you unsheathe your weapon from your belt and hold it ready in case danger should come from an unsuspected quarter.

When you reach the portal, you discover that it comprises a seamless sheet of lead-lined iron, many inches thick. You detect a lingering aura of magic around its threshold which makes you wary that a trap may have been set. Yet when you summon your psychic skills to probe deeper, you sense otherwise. You detect that Wolf's Bane has deliberately cast an illusion of magic around this portal, no doubt in the hope that it will delay or deter you long enough for the storm to do its work. Confident that the door is not lethal, you examine it more closely. Set flush into the glassy surface of its surrounding arch, you discover an inscription above two squares of dull crimson gemstone. Your sixth senses reveal that by tapping upon each square a correct number of times you will cause the door to open. Cautiously you place your fingers lightly upon the squares and feel the gentle vibration of the door's locking mechanism. By concentrating on these vibrations you hope to be able to decipher its locking codes.

After several minutes you determine that the first code is equal to the ENDURANCE points score below which a Grand Master cannot use the Discipline of Kai-surge.

The second code is equal to the number of villages that lie on the highway between the cities of Holmgard and Ragadorn.

In order to determine the numbers that will open

the door to the temple, consult the map and games rules at the front of this book. When you think you know the two-digit solution, turn to the entry that is the same number as your answer.

If you cannot decipher the codes, turn instead to **283**.

252

The moment you enter the new passage, the concealed panel slides shut behind you. Almost immediately, another panel slides out of the metal wall and seals off the passage ahead, trapping you in the cell-like space between. You throw yourself against the steel door and run your hands over its smooth surface, searching frantically for a means to escape. Your efforts are made all the more urgent when suddenly a loud hissing sound fills your ears; it is the sound of the air being extracted from this cell.

Gasping for breath, you turn around to search the opposite panel. Your hopes rise when you see a combination lock set flush into its surface. It is unlike the lock which secured the entrance to the temple of Avaros, but your Kai senses soon detect how it operates. The lock is inlaid with five dials in two groups. There is one group of three and one group of two. Each dial indicates a number. One dial however, in the group of two, is set to zero. By turning this dial to the correct number you will cause the lock to disengage.

Study the following sequence of numbers carefully.

When you think you know what the correct solution is, turn to the page that is the same as your answer.

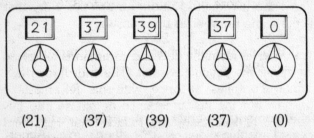

(21)   (37)   (39)   (37)   (0)

If you guess incorrectly, or if you cannot answer this puzzle, turn instead to **303**.

253

Having been detected, your immediate reaction is to bolt for the exit and, as you run, arrows whistle down to splash into the mire all around your feet. Anxious to avoid risking being hit by a second volley, you increase your pace as you approach the mouth of the tunnel.

Turn to **70**.

254

You pass through the arch and enter a long passageway that is crafted from sheets of silver and steel. A panel of translucent mineral is embedded into the entire length of the ceiling, illuminating the tunnel with a harsh phosphorescent light. You have covered several hundred yards before you see a small alcove set into the wall. A stream of clear water pours from a pipe protruding from the alcove, and drains away into a grille set into the floor. The sight and sound of the trickling water makes you thirsty for a drink.

If you wish to stop and take a drink from this
pipe, turn to **33**.

If you choose not to drink, turn to **336**.

255

Naar moves from the dais and commands Kekataag
to cease his psychic assault. The murderous lev-
iathan complies at once with his fell master's
wishes. For the first time since he strode into this
throne hall, Kekataag turns to face Naar. His intent
is to bow his huge form in dutiful deference to
his master's authority, but this formality is soon
forgotten when his psychic powers detect the presence of Alyss. The realization that she is here makes
the warrior bellow with supernatural rage. The
deafening sound galvanizes Alyss into action; she
leaps towards the plinth and places both of her
hands upon the surface of the Moonstone. Instantly
a whirling hole appears in the smoky wall of the
throne hall; it is the unmistakable mouth of a
Shadow Gate.

'Flee, Lone Wolf,' she cries, 'flee to your homeland
before it's too late!'

Bravely she stands her ground, her hands clasped
upon the glowing Moonstone, as Kekataag and
Naar advance upon her from two sides. You are
deeply moved by the courage of this enigmatic
being; it seems she is prepared to sacrifice her
immortality that you might escape alive from this
terrible place.

If you wish to obey her command and enter the
whirling Shadow Gate, turn to **282**.

If you choose to stay and fight the Dark God and
his evil avenger, turn to **343**.

256

Your advanced Kai senses detect faint magical
energies radiating from a large chunk of rubble
which lies in the open doorway to this tomb. Cautiously you move nearer to inspect the slab of stone
and discover an intricate design scratched upon its
surface. It has been smeared with dirt and a magical
spell of shielding has been placed upon it to disguise its true purpose, yet you immediately realize
what it is and you recoil from the slab, hurriedly
retreating a dozen paces. It is a glyph of power: a
magical booby trap that has been expertly camouflaged to keep it secret. If anyone or anything were
to step upon or pass over this glyph, the energy
contained within it would be released in one devastating instant.

You warn the others of what you have found and
tell them to retreat with you to a safe distance.
From the cover of a gravestone, several yards from
the tomb, you instruct Star Lynx to pick up a rock
and hurl it through the open doorway. He selects
an apple-sized chunk of granite and lobs it accurately into the tomb.

Pick a number from the *Random Number Table*.

If the number you have chosen is *1–4*, turn to
211.
If it is *5–9*, turn to **53**.

257

Your Kai mastery skills and your sheer will to survive save you from succumbing to a grisly death in this morass. After an agonizing ordeal, you finally reach the door at the end of the hall and haul yourself through it. Aching with fatigue (lose 4 ENDURANCE points), you lie on the solid flagstones for several minutes until you regain sufficient strength to be able to continue your hunt for Wolf's Bane.

You can feel a warm breeze wafting along this hall and you sense that it comes from a stairwell at the far end. When you investigate it, you rediscover Wolf's Bane's footprints on the stone steps. You cast your hands over them and detect that this is not a false trail: your enemy passed this way sometime within the last hour.

Slowly you ascend the stairs and arrive at the arched entrance to a large, vaulted stone chamber. Gathered around a fountain set into its north wall are a group of six grey-skinned humanoids. They are busy drinking a clear, oily fluid that pours from the fountain's spout into a semi-circular trough. All are barefoot and clad in rags, and they are each armed with a spear and a bow. The only exit from this chamber appears to be an archway set high in the north wall. There is a balcony in front of it that can only be reached by two flights of stairs which rise up on either side of the fountain.

Quietly you observe the creatures slaking their thirsts, and you try to formulate a way in which you can get past them and reach the balconied exit in the north wall.

If you possess a Bow, and the Discipline of Magi-

magic, and have attained the rank of Kai
Grand Guardian, turn to **138**.

If you possess Kai-alchemy and have attained
the rank of Grand Crown (and wish to use it),
turn to **26**.

If you do not possess these skills, or a Bow, or
if you have yet to attain the required levels of
Kai mastery, turn to **121**.

258

The tracks lead out of the tunnel and across a
clearing before disappearing into the jungle perimeter. Deeply suspicious, you peer through the
curtain of vines and scan along the jungle's edge
for signs of your adversary.

If you possess Grand Pathsmanship and Grand
Huntmastery, turn to **68**.

If you do not possess both of these Grand Master
Disciplines, turn to **317**.

259

A white-hot spike of pain penetrates deep into your
chest as the onrushing bolt hits you and slams
you against the moving wall of the shaft: lose 6
ENDURANCE points.

If you survive this wounding, adjust your *Action
Chart* accordingly.

To continue, turn to **37**.

260

Baron Caldar escorts you and Banedon to the roof
of his castle's main tower where, hovering above,
you see the great gleaming hull of the Guildmas-

ter's skyship – *Cloud Dancer*. At Banedon's signal a cage is lowered from the stern of this magical vessel and, after bidding farewell to the Baron, you are both hoisted aboard. The crew, some of whom are survivors from his previous skyship – *Skyrider* – are clearly agitated by your unexpected appearance; the sibilant hiss of their fearful whispers echoes softly along the deck. But immediately Banedon vouches that you are not the impostor who has terrorized Sommerlund these past few weeks and this swiftly allays his crew's suspicions. As you accompany the Guildmaster to his quarters, the mood of the men and dwarves of the ship's complement changes. Respectfully they salute you and welcome you with pride aboard their wondrous craft.

The *Cloud Dancer* sets sail and follows a south-westerly bearing for the city of Tyso, over one hundred miles distant. The night sky is clear and Javano, the ship's pilot, is confident that you will arrive within the hour. During the brief voyage, Banedon communicates magically with the elders of his Brotherhood in Toran. He informs them of your safe return and tells them of your plans to track down the impostor. In response they assure him that word of your return will be conveyed at once to the King in Holmgard, and to your beleaguered kinsmen at the Kai Monastery. This glad news does much to lift your bruised spirits.

It seems as if you have been aboard the *Cloud Dancer* for no more than a few minutes when a message arrives from the forward lookout: 'Tyso lights due south'. You leave Banedon's comfortable quarters below deck and accompany him to the prow rail from where you catch your first aerial glimpse of the distant city-port. The warm lantern-light of hovels and taverns shimmers like a captive cluster of stars within the city's protective wall. At the Guildmaster's command, Javano begins the skyship's descent and, as the twinkling lights loom larger, you are able to make out the silhouette of a grand castle that is perched on a headland overlooking the harbour.

'There's our destination, Lone Wolf,' says Bane-don, cheerfully, 'the castle of Baron Tor Medar – the Seneschal of Tyso.'

Turn to **7**.

Now you can hear the creature loping towards you. The squeal of its metal joints merges with the whirring clack of its great iron jaw. The sound unnerves you and, for a terrifying moment, your sweat-slick fingers cannot grip the disc in your tunic pocket. Then you have it and quickly you insert it into the slot in the wall.

The door opens with a hiss. You rush forward and immediately sidestep to place a solid wall between you and the steel monster. The door slides shut and, a few moments later, you feel a shudder run through the wall as the creature slams head-first into the portal and shatters its skull.

Your swift escape may have saved your life, but in your haste to evade the mechanical wolf you left behind the key which opened the portal (erase the Iron Disc from your *Action Chart*).

To continue, turn to **83**.

262

The tunnel twists and turns for several hundred yards before entering a large vault that is knee-deep in brackish grey slime. A huge black iron pot hangs suspended by a large chain in the middle of the vault, ten feet above the surface of the slimy floor. The oily chain runs around a large wheel fixed near the ceiling and drops through the centre of a slit, high up in the opposite wall. Carefully you approach the entrance to the vault and, using your Magnakai Discipline of Pathsmanship, you detect that the pot hides two creatures. They are lying in ambush. There is an exit on the far side of the vault, but in order to reach it you will have to pass directly below the hanging pot. Using the cover of shadows at the entrance to the vault, you look to the far exit and consider how you can reach it unscathed.

> If you possess the Discipline of Assimilance, and have attained the rank of Kai Grand Guardian, or higher, turn to **94**.
> If you do not possess this skill, or if you have yet to attain this level of Kai mastery, turn to **225**.

263

The creature that is diving towards you suddenly freezes in mid-air. The morbid fear of death that had gripped your heart quickly evaporates, but you are left with a feeling of deep unease as your Kai senses detect that something extraordinary is taking place around you. The hall has become filled with a deadly silence and everything, including the tongues of flame trailing from the creature's sword, and the blazing fire in the grate, is utterly frozen. It is as if time itself is standing still.

Wolf's Bane is a frozen statue, his face fixed in the malevolent sneer he was wearing in gleeful anticipation that you were about to meet your doom. You are beginning to think that perhaps you have been killed and that this is life after death, when suddenly you glimpse a blurred movement at the corner of your eye.

From out of the shadows cast by the gallery steps a young teenage girl, dressed in a leather jerkin and threadbare trousers. You recognize her at once – it is Alyss, the strange enigmatic creature who helped you once before, during your confrontation with the Demoness Shamath.

'Wh . . . what are you doing here?' you stammer. Casually she walks towards you and reaches up to touch a finger to the frozen fiery sword clutched in the taloned hands of Wolf's Bane's winged minion.

'Why, doing what I like doing best,' she replies, airily, 'minding other people's business.'

She prods the frozen sword with the tip of her finger and there is a gentle *Pop!* Instantly the creature disappears.

'I do hate cheats,' she says, as she wanders over to where Wolf's Bane is standing immobile. Cheekily she pokes out her tongue at him and then she spins on her heel to face you.

'Now, perhaps you can finish what you came here to do, Lone Wolf,' she says, and claps her hands three times. A sudden rush of noise assails your ears and your senses reel as the reality of time comes flooding back into the hall.

Turn to **296**.

264

The thick, trunk-like stamen is covered with fine hairs which help you to make the long climb towards the amber-coloured light far above. However, as you get nearer to the light, the stamen hairs become coated with lumps of sticky, sweet-smelling yellow pollen. These pollen clusters hamper your progress as you have to struggle to unglue yourself from them every time you shift your position.

You are nearing the stamen's bud-like top when you become aware of a distant buzzing sound. Rapidly the noise gets louder until you are suddenly plunged into semi-darkness. A huge winged insect is hovering directly above you, its multi-coloured body blotting out most of the pale amber sky. It lunges back and forth with its great head as it sucks away clumps of pollen from surrounding stamens with its long, spear-like proboscis. Then the creature detects your presence and the deafening noise of its wings changes pitch. It rises several feet above the stamen and hovers there for a few moments while it studies you with massive composite eyes. Unfortunately it takes only a few seconds for the creature to decide that it wants to vary its diet of pollen. With a sinister nod of its head, it extends its proboscis and then stabs its sticky point towards your unprotected back.

If you wish to attempt to defend yourself from this creature's attack, turn to **135**.

If you decide to attempt to evade it, turn to **214**.

265

You draw upon your Magnakai Discipline of Psi-screen to repel this psychic attack, but your defence is not sufficient enough to completely protect the fabric of your mind: lose 3 ENDURANCE points.

The surprise assault on your mental defences has bought this castle guardian the precious few seconds it needs in which to advance upon you. As the pain in your head recedes, you see the armoured warrior striding towards you with its sword raised high, poised ready to deal you a mighty blow.

Meghanic: COMBAT SKILL 48 ENDURANCE 48

This being is immune to all forms of psychic attack, except Kai-surge and Kai-blast.

If you win the combat, turn to **338**.

266

The arrows splash into the mire, dangerously close to where you are standing. You sense that the volley was not aimed at you; it was let loose in the hope of hitting you by chance. You suspect that the creatures who fired these arrows have an exceptional hearing ability, and rather than risk them getting lucky with their second volley, you decide to throw caution to the wind and make a dash for the exit tunnel.

Turn to **309**.

267

There is no door to the entrance of this derelict dwelling and, after checking that Wolf's Bane has left no unwelcome surprises, you enter and find a foyer strewn with mouldering masonry. Two stair-cases lead off this small entrance hall; one ascends to the floor above, the other descends to the base-ment. The stairwell down is blocked by timbers and sheets of crumpled iron. It shows no signs of having been disturbed for years and so you choose instead to explore the upper floor.

At the top of the stairs you make an unexpected discovery. You emerge into a corridor that is lined with a seamless metallic skin. Unlike the dereliction you have so far witnessed, the walls and floor of this passage bear no signs of neglect or corrosion. They gleam like highly polished steel.

You explore the corridor and come to what, at first sight, appears to be a dead end. Then you hear a loud hiss and a concealed panel slides open to reveal another steel-lined passageway. You pause to examine the panel but you can detect no traps or residues of magic.

If you wish to enter the new passageway, turn to **252**.

If you choose not to enter, turn to **274**.

268

The buttress and the rope plummet into the fissure and are lost to an underground river far below. For a few terrible seconds Steel Hand swings precariously from the ceiling, then his fingers lose their purchase and he, too, tumbles into the abyss.

You and your young Kai comrades rush to the edge of the fissure, fearing the worst. But Steel Hand has not fallen into the raging river to be carried out to sea; he is still in sight. Your infravision reveals him to be lying on a rocky ledge less than twenty feet below. He has been knocked unconscious by the fall but thankfully he is still alive.

It takes nearly an hour to retrieve Steel Hand from the ledge and then cross safely to the far side of the fissure. During this time, unless you possess Grand Huntmastery, you must eat a Meal or lose 3 ENDURANCE points.

'Come, my lords,' you say, mindful of the unwelcome dangers and delays you have so far endured, 'we must press on. We've yet to find our quarry's trail.'

Turn to **160**.

269

With mounting dread, you watch as the seconds tick away. When the illuminated display reaches zero, there is a sun-like burst of light which totally obliterates your senses; it is the last light that you ever see. The bomb detonates and explodes with terrific force, destroying the dragonfly pens and several of the upper storeys of the tower.

Sadly, your struggle against Wolf's Bane has ended in defeat, leaving the way clear for Naar's forces to invade and conquer Magnamund. Your life and your duel end here.

270

Hurriedly you spit out the words of the Brotherhood spell *Invisible Shield* and sweep your hand in a circle before your face. You complete the spell barely seconds before the deadly shaft splinters against this magical protection and falls in pieces to the ground.

Turn to **133**.

271

Your search uncovers many interesting and rare items, but few which are of any practical value. The only item worthy of consideration is a valuable goblet, crafted from gold. (If you wish to take and keep this Gold Cup, record it on your *Action Chart* as a Special Item.)

To continue, turn to **12**.

272

You recite the words' of the Brotherhood spell *Strength*, and feel a wave of vibrant energy course through your body and limbs. Charged with the power of this spell, you take a firm grip of the portcullis with both hands and lift with all your might. The heavy iron portal creaks and shudders, then its hidden counterweights bow to your efforts. The portal rises and you are able to make a swift escape from the clutches of the chained serpent.

You retrace your steps along the tunnel, passing the place where you first appeared in this subterranean labyrinth, and continue on until you reach a large vault that is knee-deep in brackish grey slime. A huge black iron pot hangs suspended by a large chain in the middle of the vault, ten feet above the surface of the slimy floor. The oily chain runs around a large wheel fixed near the ceiling and drops through the centre of a slit, high up in the opposite wall. Carefully you approach the entrance to the vault and, using your Magnakai Discipline of Pathsmanship, you detect that the pot hides two creatures. They are lying in ambush. There is an exit on the far side of the vault, but in order to reach it you will have to pass directly below the hanging pot. Using the cover of shadows at the entrance to the vault, you look to the far exit and consider how you can reach it unscathed.

If you possess the Discipline of Assimilance, and have attained the rank of Kai Grand Guardian, or higher, turn to **94**.

If you do not possess this skill, or if you have yet to attain this level of Kai mastery, turn to **225**.

273

You feel your throat tightening as the air is sucked out of the chamber. The whirling flames of the fire have rapidly transformed into a raging vortex which is dragging into its core every loose item in the banquet hall. You and Alyss hang on to the banister rail affixed to the gallery stairs, but it is becoming increasingly difficult to maintain your grip. Chairs, tapestries, tables and other furniture batter you as they tumble past to be sucked into the vortex (lose 2 ENDURANCE points). Then the rail collapses and the two of you are drawn into the raging heart of this fearsome whirlpool.

Turn to **170**.

274

You return to the stairs and descend to the foyer.
Mindful of your enemy's skills of deception and
illusion, you take a closer look at the debris which
blocks the stairs leading down. But you cannot
detect any tracks or evidence that Wolf's Bane has
come this way. You are about to abandon the
stairwell and leave the building when something
catches your eye. Protruding from the dust that
covers the top step is a small disc of iron engraved
with runic symbols. (If you wish to keep this Iron
Disc, record it on your *Action Chart* as a Special
Item.)

To leave the building and continue, turn to **71**.

275

Lining the walls of this passage are countless thousands of small alcoves, each one occupied by the
skull of an ancient Tysoan. Occasionally this
macabre display is punctuated by a sealed tomb or
burial urn, but in the main the parade of mirthless
skulls seems to go on forever.

At length you come to a circular vault where, unexpectedly, you can hear the sound of the sea. Using
your infravision to scan the dark chamber before
entering, you note that a wide section of its stone
floor has collapsed. The sound of the sea breaking
against a distant shoreline wells up from this gaping
hollow.

With caution guiding your step, you enter the inky-
black chamber and inch your way to the edge of
the fissure. You can detect no living creatures or

other sources of heat, but using your Kai senses you are able to determine that the hollow is more than one hundred feet deep. There is one exit from the vault, but it lies over forty feet away, on the opposite side of the fissure.

If you possess Kai-alchemy, and wish to use it, turn to **66**.

If you do not possess this skill, or if you choose not to use it, turn to **247**.

276

You make your way towards the avenue and select an ideal place from where you can launch an ambush. Twenty minutes tick by before you see two armoured humanoids approaching. One walks several paces behind the other, but both are on their way towards the tower. At first you are discouraged that there are two, fearing that an ambush will be harder to effect. But as they draw closer you note that neither appears to be carrying weapons.

You let the first warrior pass and then you strike the second one, dragging him off the street and into the dark alley where you have been lying in wait. A sharp blow beneath the chin-guard of his helmet renders him unconscious, and swiftly you begin to strip away his armour. All is going to plan until a scraping noise behind alerts you to trouble. His companion has noticed that he is alone and has retraced his steps to investigate the sudden disappearance of his brother-in-arms.

You are holding an armoured breastplate in both hands when he comes striding into the alley. You

XV. The warrior bats your weapon aside and attempts to close his hands around your throat.

hurl it at him, hoping to buy yourself a few precious seconds in which you can unsheathe your weapon, but the warrior bats it aside and attempts to close his hands around your throat.

Manoyd (with power gloves):
COMBAT SKILL 40 ENDURANCE 40

Unless you possess Grand Weaponmastery, and have attained the rank of Grand Crown, you must reduce your COMBAT SKILL by four for the duration of this fight.

If you win the combat, turn to **289**.

277

You speak the words of the Brotherhood spell *Lightning Hand* and point your right index finger at the iron pot. There is a flash of bluish light and then an arc of crackling electricity leaps from your finger to strike the top of the pot, blowing a fist-sized chunk of rusty iron out of its turned rim. One of the creatures is killed instantly by the blast and the other is stunned when the electrical charge is earthed along the supporting chain.

You sense that the surviving creature is only temporarily incapacitated; it will soon revive and it will be sure to attempt to avenge its dead companion by shooting at you with its bow. Mindful of the pending danger, you hurriedly examine the portal for a lever or some other means to make it rise.

Turn to **18**.

278

You escape through the steel roof of the tower and

catch a fleeting glimpse of the rainswept city far below. Suddenly there is a tremendous flash, followed almost immediately by the concussive blast from an enormous explosion. A debris-laden shockwave hits you from behind, flattens you against the dragonfly's crusty neck, and leaves you bleeding from several minor wounds: lose 2 ENDURANCE points.

Fortunately your winged mount survives the shockwave unscathed and is propelled upwards at greater speed into the base of the thick storm clouds.

Turn to **310**.

279

You press the index finger of your right hand against the plant wall and whisper the words of the Brotherhood spell *Lightning Hand*. You feel a tingling sensation run down your arm and then a crackling flame ignites at your fingertip which burns a neat hole through the stem. Then, quite suddenly, the sap within the plant wall catches fire and within seconds you find yourself trapped inside a roaring cocoon of fire.

The highly flammable sap feeds the flames, and the temperature rapidly increases until the inside of the stem becomes as hot as a blazing furnace. Unless you possess the Discipline of Grand Nexus, you lose 5 ENDURANCE points before the flames die down and you are able to burst free from the smouldering stem.

To continue, turn to **230**.

'Come, Grand Master. You're going home,' she says, and she takes you by the hand and leads you to the middle of the banquet hall, to a place directly opposite the great fireplace. 'But first we must make preparations for the journey.'

Alyss then proceeds to tell you to use your advanced Kai mastery to mask the goodly aura that radiates naturally from your mind and body. Having done as she requests, she touches the platinum amulet which you wear around your neck and smiles.

'Good, good,'she enthuses, 'this bauble will take care of the rest.'

She then takes a piece of limestone from her pocket and proceeds to draw a pentagram on the floor of the hall. She has half-completed the complicated design when suddenly she becomes agitated.

'Must hurry,' she mumbles, 'must, must hurry.'

Suddenly the fire in the hearth flares brightly. The flames begin to grow and whirl and slowly change colour.

'It's no good!' cries Alyss, tearful with frustration. Angrily she casts her chunk of crumbling limestone at the roaring flames and then leaps to her feet and comes rushing to your side. 'It's too late!' she screams, her voice now barely audible above the unnatural crackling of the fire, 'Naar is summoning his champion!'

Pick a number from the *Random Number Table*.

XVI. 'It's too late!' screams Alyss. 'Naar is summoning his champion!'

If the number you have picked is *0–4*, turn to **273**.

If it is *5–9*, turn to **67**.

281

You draw upon all of your defensive Kai Disciplines to protect you from the effects of the vortex. The agony abates, but the effort depletes your reserves of mental and physical stamina: lose 5 ENDURANCE points.

As the pain melts, so the strands of light unravel themselves and dissolve. As the silvery cloud disappears, you find yourself plummeting ever nearer to the blazing heart of this cosmic whirlpool. Then, at the moment you plunge into its core, your senses are obliterated and you are engulfed by a total darkness.

From out of the depths of this cold dark universe there appears a pinpoint of light. You feel yourself being drawn inexorably towards it and, although you struggle to resist, you cannot tear yourself free from its irresistible pull. You feel yourself accelerating towards it until the speck becomes as large as a glowing sun. Then, with an abruptness that leaves you gasping, there is a flash of blue-white light and you find yourself lying spread-eagled upon a bed of moist green foliage.

Turn to **49**.

282

Desperately you scramble across the throne hall and leap towards the swirling maw of this supernatural portal, but your entry is barred by a horde of shrieking horrors which materialize from the smoke surrounding the circumference of the Shadow Gate. Immediately you recognize them and your heart sinks – they are Crypt Spawn.

Now Naar himself is aware of your true identity and he is determined not to let you escape from the Plane of Darkness.

If you possess the Sommerswerd, turn to **3**.
If you do not possess this Special Item, turn to **123**.

283

Unable to decipher the code, you decide instead to attempt to dismantle the locking mechanism. Using the buckle of your belt, you work it between the gemstone lockplates and attempt to prise them away. It is a difficult and delicate procedure, made doubly so by the increasing ferocity of the storm which is tearing through the fabric of your cloak and tunic: lose 3 ENDURANCE points.

After several painful minutes you succeed in lifting off the gemstone plates. But this does not release the locking mechanism; it simply exposes it to the elements. In order to force the door to open you must now physically destroy the exposed mechanism.

Temple Portal: COMBAT SKILL 50 ENDURANCE 50

Conduct a combat in the usual manner. Any ENDURANCE points lost by yourself result from the effects of prolonged exposure to the storm.

If you succeed in reducing the door's ENDURANCE

score to zero before losing all of your own, turn to **157**.

284

Nimbly you dodge aside, but droplets of the creature's drool splash your arm and shoulder to burn straight through your tunic with frightening speed. You immediately call upon your Magnakai Discipline of Nexus for protection against this acidic saliva, but the substance is highly corrosive and your innate skill is hard-pressed to provide you with adequate protection.

Pick a number from the *Random Number Table* (0=10). The resultant score is equal to the number of ENDURANCE points you lose due to the effects of this acid on your skin and muscle.

If you wish to attack the creature that has spat at you, turn to **141**.

If you wish to evade this creature, turn to **91**.

285

Warily you approach the settlement, your keen senses absorbing every detail. The line of deserted mud huts look innocuous, but the words of the voice of Naar still linger in your memory. This humid jungle realm lies within his domain; it is therefore reasonable to expect the inhabitants of this place to be wholly devoted to the cause of Evil.

You reach the edge of the undergrowth and pause to assess potential threats. The huts are semi-derelict, all bearing some signs of neglect and decay. The clay-tiled hovel that Wolf's Bane

entered appears to be empty, but when you focus upon its open doorway, you see what appears to be a trench cut into the earth. You magnify your vision and at once you see steps in the wall of this excavation. Your heart sinks: Wolf's Bane has escaped underground.

If you wish to enter the hut and follow your enemy without further delay, turn to **161**.

If you choose to investigate the hut to check for traps, turn to **188**.

286

Obediently, Black Hawk stands aside. You cast your eyes over the surface of the north wall for one last time, to satisfy yourself that you can detect no lurking traps, and when you are fully confident that it is safe you take up your weapon and put it to the crack in the wall. Because you are so sure that there is no threat, what occurs in the next instant is doubly shocking.

You press forward with all of your weight yet, unexpectedly, you meet with no resistance. Your weapon disappears into the wall and you stumble forward to plunge through seemingly solid granite. For a second or two you are consumed by total darkness, then an explosion of white light obliterates your vision and you feel yourself being hurled backwards by a searing wave of heat.

Pick a number from the *Random Number Table* (0=10). Now add 2 to the number you have picked. The resultant total is the number of ENDURANCE points you have lost as a consequence of this explosion.

Make the appropriate adjustment to your *Action Chart* and continue by turning to **154**.

287

As you climb the stairs, you are filled with a growing sense of uncertainty and dread as you ponder what may yet await you in this alien tower. However, these feelings of impending doom are quickly banished when you reach the third level, for here you pick up the trail of your adversary. Your tracking skills determine that his trail is fresh and you pursue it eagerly.

You pass through a maze of empty passageways which lead eventually to a large, circular hall. Cautiously you approach the entrance and peer inside. Your tracking skills and your curiosity are handsomely rewarded when you see Wolf's Bane; he is standing alone and he is unaware that you have found him.

Turn to **100**.

288

Quickly you take the incendiary from your Backpack, prime its crude detonator, and hurl it at the hanging cauldron. There is a splash of oily yellow flame as it impacts and smashes against the lip of the iron pot, then, in a terrifying instant, the two reptilians are consumed in a roaring ball of fire. You watch with shocked fascination as they shriek their last and tumble from the pot to splash, like two fiery meteors, into the mire.

You turn your eyes away from the terrible sight and, to your amazement, you see the portal beginning to rise of its own accord. You wait until it has risen a few feet and you are sure that no enemy awaits you on the other side, then you duck under the heavy iron plate and hurry into the tunnel beyond. As you run, you hear the portal slamming shut behind you with a dull reverberating boom, sealing away the smouldering remains of your two would-be assassins.

Turn to **115**.

289

You drag the body of the dead Manoyd into the ruins of a house and cover it with rubble. Then you put on the armour, which you have stripped from the unconscious Manoyd, and lower the visor of the helmet to hide your face. A black haversack taken from the warrior provides you with a convenient means to hide your own weapons, equipment, and cloak.

After checking that the avenue is clear, you emerge

from the alley and stride boldly towards the tower. On reaching the edge of this windswept canyon, you hear the distant clang of a bell and watch as the drawbridge extends from beneath the portal to span the chasm. You march across, trying not to look down through the semi-transparent bridge to the dark floor of the moat that lies thousands of feet below, and enter the tower's great portal.

Turn to **124**.

Turn to **124**.

290

Your experienced eye is drawn to the chamber's north wall. You step closer and magnify your vision, which enables you to detect two faint hairline cracks in the damp granite surface. They run vertically from the floor to the ceiling and appear to be the outline of a secret panel. But all is not what it seems. You utter the words of the advanced Brotherhood spell *See Illusion*, and the truth is swiftly revealed. The panel does not exist: it is a skilful illusion. With the memory of the powerglyph you encountered at the tomb entrance still fresh in your mind, you command your companions to stand with their backs against the south wall. Then you scoop a handful of gravel from the floor and hurl it at the north wall. There is a sudden flash of blue-white light which melts into a shower of hissing sparks as the gravel passes through the illusory panel, dissipating its energy.

'Just as I thought – another trick!' you say, as you unsheathe your weapon and signal to your comrades to follow your lead. 'Be on your guard, my lords. We're hunting a cunning foe.'

Turn to **345**.

291

Unfortunately your attempt to evade this magical missile is unsuccessful. A white-hot spike of pain penetrates deep into your chest as the onrushing bolt hits you and slams you against the moving wall of the shaft: lose 6 ENDURANCE points.

If you survive this wounding, adjust your *Action Chart* accordingly.

To continue, turn to **37**.

292

You extend your right arm and point your hand at the stone trough. Then you speak the words of the Brotherhood spell *Lightning Hand* and a familiar tingle rushes along your arm to explode into life at the tip of your index finger. A bolt of blue fire arcs towards the trough and, with a deafening *wumph!*, it ignites the liquid to create a blazing fireball. Greedily, this guttering ball of flame consumes the creatures who are gathered around the lip of the trough.

Turn to **204**.

293

You concentrate upon the entrance to the tunnel as you recite the words of the Brotherhood spell *Teleport*. You feel a power building deep within your body, a power you are able to contain until the moment comes to release it. As soon as the writhing giant serpent twists away from the tunnel mouth, you channel the spell's energy into propelling you across the cavern. Within seconds you are able to reach the safety of the exit and make your escape unscathed.

Use of this spell drains you of 5 ENDURANCE points. Make the necessary adjustment to your *Action Chart* before continuing.

Turn to **115**.

Less than a hundred paces along this tunnel you come to a narrow hall which is lined with shelves. These thin and ancient beams sag under the weight of a strange collection of bones, stones, shells, ornaments and other curios. The uppermost shelves are crowded with books, all old, dusty and damaged.

You are advancing past the shelves, towards a door at the end of the hall, when a strange sound makes you freeze in your tracks. Something is moving behind the books on the top shelf. You tilt your head to look and find yourself staring into the corpse-green eyes of a round, pudding-shaped creature. It seems to be smiling, but then it purses its bulbous lips and spits a stream of smoky-coloured fluid at your face.

Pick a number from the *Random Number Table*. If you possess Grand Huntmastery, add 2 to the number you have picked.

If your total is now 4 or less, turn to **284**.
If it is 5 or higher, turn to **117**.

295

The creature's sharp proboscis penetrates your Backpack and gouges a furrow of skin from your ribs: lose 3 ENDURANCE points.

Before it can strike again, you prise yourself out of the sticky cluster and retreat back along the stamen until you are out of harm's way. Excited by the taste of your warm blood, the giant insect stabs and slashes wildly, splintering stamen tips and drenching you with showers of sticky pollen. Fortunately, the span of its gigantic wings and the narrowness of the plant's corolla conspire to prevent it from reaching deeper into the plant and you are able to escape without sustaining further injuries.

Turn to **305**.

296

The triumphant sneer dies on Wolf's Bane's face the instant he realizes that his winged minion has disappeared and that you are still alive. He recoils, his mouth gaping and his eyes wide with disbelief. As he retreats, he brushes against Alyss and utters a yelp of fright. His abject fear, however, soon transforms into blind fury.

'You!' he cries, accusingly. Fuelled by rage, he raises his sword in readiness to slash at her face. You rush forward and block his vicious blow, then you twist the blade from his grasp and, with one swift thrust, you skewer his heart upon the tip of your rapier.

Wolf's Bane regards the blade protruding from his chest with a look of utter astonishment. Then, with a curse on his blood-flecked lips, he drops to his knees and crumples lifelessly to the floor.

Turn to **40**.

297

Warily you approach the settlement, your keen senses absorbing every detail. The line of deserted mud huts look innocuous but the words of the voice of Naar still linger in your memory. This humid jungle realm lies within his domain; it is therefore reasonable to expect that the inhabitants of this place will be wholly devoted to the cause of Evil.

You reach the edge of the undergrowth and pause to assess potential threats. The huts are semi-derelict, all bearing some signs of neglect and decay. The nearest one is a clay-tiled hovel that, like the others, appears to be empty. But when you focus upon its open doorway you see that a trench has been cut into its earth floor. You magnify your vision and at once you detect steps in the wall of this excavation, leading underground.

If you wish to enter the hut and investigate where these steps lead to, turn to **161**.

If you choose instead to check the hut for traps, turn to **27**.

298

This tunnel gradually descends by slope and stair through deeper levels of the catacombs. You detect no trace of the impostor and, when eventually the tunnel comes to a dead end, you curse your ill luck and turn reluctantly to retrace your steps. It is then that you sense a faint but lingering aura of evil close to the tunnel floor.

Closer inspection reveals a trapdoor set into the flagstones. You pull this heavy hatch open and discover a circulate chute and a ladder descending into darkness. Your heart misses a beat when you notice fresh tracks on the ladder's iron rungs; at last you have found the impostor's trail.

Cautiously you lead the descent into the chute, using your powers of infravision to scan for signs of movement in the damp darkness below. After several minutes you reach the bottom of the ladder where you discover a large vaulted chamber. Around its walls are positioned urns and grey stone caskets, each embellished with traces of gold. There is an unexpected air of opulence about this vault which prompts you to guess that it is a secret burial tomb.

If you have ever visited the Graveyard of the Ancients in a previous *Lone Wolf* adventure, turn to **182**.

If you have never visited this place, turn to **206**.

299

Your arrow hits its mark and penetrates deep into the creature's eye socket. There is a splash of white sparks and a crackle of electrical arcing as the tip punches through the back of its steel skull, and yet the beast comes on. The wound has inflicted serious damage to its sight and senses, but it does not stop it from pressing home its attack. You have barely one second remaining in which to unsheathe a hand weapon as this great metallic horror launches itself at your chest.

Mech-wulf: COMBAT SKILL 38 ENDURANCE 35

This creature is immune to all psychic attacks.

If you win this combat, turn to **5**.

300

From the uppermost reaches of the tower there descends an icy fog which radiates an intensely powerful aura of evil. This menacing mist darkens as it swirls around the lower levels, like some huge vaporous snake seeking out its prey. Then, slowly, it gathers in towards the centre of the chamber where it hangs above the plinth like an angry thunderhead, roiling and seething with colossal malevolence.

You gaze into this black cloud and are gripped by an abject terror the instant you fathom its nature and purpose. This cloud is not of this world and it has not fully taken on substance and being within the material plane of Aon, yet even in its malformed state you recognize it to be a materialization of ultimate evil. This is a manifestation of Naar – the King of the Darkness!

Suddenly a deafening clap of thunder shakes the walls and the base of the tower is lit up by crackling arcs of lightning. The freezing air seethes with tension as the presence of Naar triggers explosive chemical imbalances within it. Then, above the crackling cacophony of noise, you hear a chilling voice speaking to you in your native tongue.

'Disciple of Kai – you know my name. Will you not deign to speak it?'

Morbid terror is ripping at your insides yet you refuse to show the slightest trace of weakness. You steel yourself and inwardly you pray to Kai and Ishir to protect you in this hour of deepest need.

'No!' you scream, 'I will never acknowledge you!'

'You may be one of Kai's favourite minions,' retorts the voice, 'but you will always be mortal. You would do well to remember that in my presence.' Thunder booms and the floor shakes beneath your feet, causing you to fall involuntarily to your knees.

'Now that you bow before me, Lone Wolf, I shall impart to you your fate, for I am the true master of Aon. This is Avaros, a small and insignificant satellite of Duron, a world that has long been devoted to my cause. And you have been lured here for one purpose – to be destroyed. During the speck of time that you have existed, you have become an impertinent obstacle to my conquest of Magnamund. For this you will forfeit your soul. Yet, before I claim your worthless soul, I shall make sport of your demise so that Kai and Ishir shall see the worthlessness of their creations and know the futility of their cause.'

Once more the thunder booms and you are blinded momentarily by a flash of white fire. Slowly your sight returns, and now you can see your adversary – Wolf's Bane – standing upon the plinth, directly below the menacing black cloud.

'Here is my champion,' speaks the voice of Naar,

'you and he are well-matched for the contest that is about to commence.'

Wolf's Bane unsheathes his sword and levels it at your chest. His facial features twist into a grotesque parody of your own as he spits out a venomous threat:

'Victory will be mine, Lone Wolf. Evil shall ultimately triumph!'

You shout a defiant riposte, but the voice of Naar booms once more, drowning your worthy cry:

'So be it! Let the duel begin!'

Turn to **30**.

301

You sprint towards the speeding wagon and hurl yourself towards its open cargo bay. But, disastrously, you misjudge your leap and crash headlong into the side of the hover-wagon, knocking yourself unconscious.

The concussion you have sustained does not kill you, but it contributes indirectly to your death. Your body is seen lying in the avenue by Wolf's Bane, from one of the tower's many watching posts, and he immediately dispatches a troop of Manoyds to capture and slay you. Sadly, they are brutally efficient servants and they obey his commands to the letter.

Tragically, your life and your duel end here.

302

'Release him, my lord,' says Banedon. The Baron,

unnerved by the sudden disappearance of the magical shield and the Guildmaster's unexpected request, takes a step backwards and reaches for his sword.

'Have no fear,' says Banedon, staying the Baron's hand, 'for we have here the real Grand Master of the Kai.'

'How can you be so sure?' retorts Caldar, his voice full of scepticism.

'I'm certain,' says Banedon, 'yet there is one way we can be absolutely sure.'

So saying, Banedon removes from the pocket of his robe a small platinum disc which is strung upon a loop of braided cord. He approaches you and slips the cord over your head.

'Here is proof,' he says. 'No agent of Naar could tolerate the touch of this goodly artifact. Banish your doubts, my lord. This man is Lone Wolf.'

(Record this Platinum Amulet, which you wear around your neck, as a Special Item on your *Action Chart*. You need not discard another item in its favour if you already possess the maximum number permissible.)

To continue, turn to **88**.

303

Within thirty seconds of both panels closing, all of the air is sucked out of this tiny metal cell. Your Magnakai Discipline of Nexus sustains you for a further ten minutes, during which precious little time you try everything possible to extricate yourself from this deadly vacuum. Unfortunately, your valiant efforts are to no avail. You are unable to penetrate the strange metal skin of this cell. Slowly, reluctantly, you succumb to the lack of oxygen until you drift off into a sleep from which you never awaken.

Sadly, your life and your duel end here.

304

Slowly you descend the stairs and approach the banqueting table. Wolf's Bane slides the open case towards you and motions for you to take a weapon. You reach for the box and remove the uppermost rapier, then you slide the case back across the table to your opponent.

'Very well,' he says, as he takes the remaining sword and makes a few strokes to gauge its balance, 'let the duel begin.'

The Duel: Lone Wolf vs. Wolf's Bane

The combat ratio for the duel is −4. This ratio

takes account of all bonuses which may apply (eg Grand Weaponmastery with Sword, psychic attacks, and Special Items). Wolf's Bane's ENDURANCE score is identical to your current ENDURANCE score, unless you possess a Bronze Disc. If you possess this Special Item, you may reduce your enemy's ENDURANCE by 4 points before the commencement of combat.

Conduct the combat using the normal combat procedure. However, should Wolf's Bane's ENDURANCE be reduced to 10 or less, do not continue any further with the fight. Instead, turn immediately to **151**.

305

You retreat all the way down to the bowl of the corolla, to where you began your ascent. Here you take the opportunity to check your Backpack and you discover that three items have been damaged beyond repair (erase three items of your choice from your current list of Backpack Items). Having had your hopes of escape thwarted by the creature, you see that the hollow stem is now the only remaining chance you have of getting out of this plant alive.

Turn to **103**.

306

You approach the hut and crouch down beside its mud wall, close to its open door. Your senses detect no glyphs or other traps here, and there are no residues of magical energy that might betray the presence of illusions or shielding spells. Wary of further delay, you approach the trench at the centre of the hut and descend a flight of steps that leads down to an underground tunnel. You still cannot detect any traps, yet you have gone only a few yards along this narrow passageway when you hear the terrifying roar of a large cat. With an abruptness that takes your breath away, a huge tiger-like beast comes bounding from out of the darkness ahead. So sudden and unexpected is this creature's attack, that you only just have time in which to unsheathe a hand-weapon as it hurls itself upon you.

Rahjaz: COMBAT SKILL 48 ENDURANCE 41

This creature is immune to all forms of psychic attack, except Kai-surge and Kai-blast.

If you win this combat, turn to **249**.

307

Your powerful Discipline of Animal Control suppresses the Bangrol's natural instinct to defend its nest and immediately it breaks off its attack. It circles around the chamber, cawing with frustration, and then re-enters the chimney and escapes back to the surface.

Turn to **78**.

308

For two hours you observe the tower. During this time you sense that an invisible field of energy surrounds the wall, a defence that augments the terrifyingly deep moat. This force field disappears only when the portal opens and the drawbridge extends to allow for the arrival or departure of armoured warriors, or strange horseless wagons that hover a few feet from the ground, but in the main the great door remains firmly closed.

You notice that the sparse traffic of warriors and wagons passes along one avenue. It is the only thoroughfare approaching the tower which has been cleared of debris. It is an uncomfortable vigil, but the time you spend observing the tower is rewarded when a bold plan gradually takes form in your mind.

You assess that an entry to the tower could be effected by two means: if you were able to ambush a warrior and use his armour as a disguise, or, if you were able to stow away aboard one of the wagons approaching the moat.

If you wish to attempt to ambush one of the armoured warriors, turn to **276**.
If you decide to attempt to stow away aboard a hover-wagon, turn to **79**.

309

You are within ten feet of the exit tunnel when a heavy sheet of iron falls from the ceiling and seals off your chosen route of escape. The fog is beginning to thin out and you can now see the creatures in the pot who attempted to shoot you full of arrows. They are small, blue-skinned reptilians, with cruel crocodilian faces and curiously human hands. They are armed with finely crafted bows of gleaming white bone that you detect are capable of discharging six poisoned arrows every second. The reptilians are close to reloading these bows — you must act quickly if you are to avoid becoming the target of a second deadly volley.

310

If you possess Kai-alchemy, and wish to use it, turn to **277**.

If you possess Magi-magic, and wish to use it, turn to **219**.

If you possess a Bow, and wish to use it, turn to **136**.

If you possess neither of these Disciplines, or a Bow, or choose to use none of them, turn to **82**.

310

The moment you pass through the storm clouds, you enter a stratosphere that is bathed with magnificent light. Above the city's perpetual cloud layer lies a wondrous vista, an aerial realm that is calm and clear. The golden rays from two suns, and the reflected light from twelve satellite moons, combine to bathe the thunderheads with a panoply of colour. You scan these heavens and see high above the dragonfly which is carrying Wolf's Bane. It is climbing towards a castle-like fortress which seems to rest upon a base of wispy cloud, defying gravity. Your enemy's flying mount enters the castle from below, passing through a gap in the underside of its cloudy base. Upon seeing his destination you urge your own winged mount to follow in his wake.

You enter the clouds and pass through an open portal, like some massive trapdoor located in the belly of this mystical stronghold. Beyond the portal is a cavern of stone, vaulted and substantial like the dungeons of a great castle. There is no sign of your enemy, save for his mount which is tethered to a wooden pier. You bring your dragonfly in to

XVII. Wolf's Bane's dragonfly enters the castle and you
       urge your own mount to follow.

land upon this pier and then leap down from its back and examine the ground for tracks. You find what you are seeking and they lead you to an archway that opens upon a landing where three tunnels lead off in different directions. However, to your dismay, you discover that Wolf's Bane has deliberately spoiled his tracks; his footprints lead to all three tunnels.

If you wish to explore the north tunnel, turn to **294**.

If you choose to explore the east tunnel, turn to **109**.

If you decide instead to explore the west tunnel, turn to **235**.

311

Desperately you take cover behind a pollen cluster as the insect's lance-like proboscis comes hurtling towards your body.

Solyx: COMBAT SKILL 45 ENDURANCE 40

This creature is immune to all forms of psychic attack, except Kai-surge and Kai-blast.

You may evade this combat after four rounds by turning to **144**.

If you win the fight, turn to **186**.

312

You dive to the ground, but the white beam is lightning fast and it glances your shoulder as you fall: lose 5 ENDURANCE points. You bite your lip to stifle a scream of pain as you hit the warehouse floor, then you scramble for the nearest cover – a heavy iron chest, banded and riveted with steel –

to avoid leaving yourself exposed to another blast from this deadly weapon. The warrior follows your swift move and discharges a second beam from his spear which slams into the iron chest with stunning force. You gasp with horror as you see the side of the chest bulging towards your face. Its thick rivets tremble and its age-blackened skin smoulders with a sullen heat. Instinct takes over, making you roll away from the iron chest and seek cover elsewhere. As you move, the beam of light tears through the rear of the iron box and destroys the ground where, only moments before, your face had been.

You call upon all of your camouflage skills to mask your body as you hurriedly seek a way to escape from this warrior and his sorcerous weapon. You reach the base of a large steel tank and scramble up a ladder fixed to its side. The top of the tank is stacked high with coiled ropes and you force yourself in amongst them. A few moments later you watch the warrior approach the smouldering remains of the iron chest. He is close enough now for you to see that his weapon is attached by a length of steel cable to a canister strapped to his back.

If you possess a Bow and the Discipline of Magi-magic, and have attained the Kai rank of Sun Lord, turn to **209**.

If you do not possess a Bow or this skill, or if you have yet to attain the rank of Sun Lord, turn to **156**.

313

As you move across the vault, you hear your

would-be ambushers moving around in the cauldron above. You are near the centre of this dingy chamber, level with the hanging pot, when a glassy sphere filled with white liquid is dropped over the side. As it hits the slimy floor it explodes, spraying droplets of the white fluid in every direction. You are hit by this fine spray which instantly reveals your position to the creatures above.

Pick a number from the *Random Number Table*. If you possess Grand Huntmastery and Assimilance, add 2 to the number you have picked.

If your total score is now *3* or less, turn to **197**.
If it is *4* or higher, turn to **253**.

314

You summon all of your Kai skills to mask your body before setting foot into the hall. You keep close to the left wall and, as you inch your way closer to the stairs, you pray that your camouflage skills will keep you hidden from the eyes of the creatures who are gathered around the trough.

Pick a number from the *Random Number Table*. If you possess Assimilance, add 3 to the number you have picked.

If your total score is *4* or lower, turn to **193**.
If it is *5* or higher, turn to **24**.

315

You gather your psychic defences and construct a wall around your mind to protect yourself from this agonizing mental assault. Your strategy is swiftly effective and costs you but a fraction of your remaining reserve of psychic energy (lose 1 ENDUR-ANCE point).

This psychic assault has been one of the strongest you have ever experienced. You have survived it, but your Kai senses tell you that your ordeal has not ended; it has only just begun. You force open your eyes and look with dread at the terrible threat that confronts you now.

Turn to **300**.

316

Beyond the net you rediscover your opponent's tracks. They lead you to an unlit storage chamber containing dozens of iron canisters and large steel crates. Using your ability to see in the dark, you follow his footprints as they wend their way around these obstacles and trail off towards a distant door. But before you reach the door you are brought to an abrupt halt by a strange sound – a whirring, mechanical growl. Instinctively you look over your shoulder, in the direction of the noise, and freeze with shock the moment you catch sight of the creature that is moving slowly towards your back.

Turn to **199**.

317

You scan the jungle perimeter several times but you can detect nothing potentially hostile lurking amongst the undergrowth and trees. You decide to follow the tracks to see where they lead and, as you emerge from the tunnel, the oppressive jungle heat hits you like a sledgehammer. Your Magnakai Discipline of Nexus automatically regulates your body temperature, making the heat bearable, yet even so it comes as a shock that any living creature can exist in this hellish environment.

Unfortunately, the shock of the jungle heat is only the first of two nasty surprises that await you. The second is a barbed arrow that whistles from out of the dense foliage and comes speeding towards your forehead!

> If you possess Kai-alchemy, and have attained the rank of Sun Knight or higher, turn to **152**.
>
> If you possess Kai-alchemy but have yet to reach this level of Kai mastery, turn to **270**.
>
> If you do not possess this Grand Master Discipline, turn to **232**.

318

Your Kai sixth sense reveals to you traces of a magical energy which is lingering around the entrance to the tomb. Your fellow Kai also detect that something is wrong, although their senses are not as finely tuned as your own and they are unable to pinpoint its source.

'Is it safe to enter, Grand Master?' whispers Steel Hand.

'I cannot be certain,' you reply, uneasily. 'But of one thing I am sure – the impostor has already descended into the catacombs by way of this entrance.'

You take a few steps back from the open tomb and point to a patch of soft earth amongst the rubble.

'Look here – it's a footprint.' You examine it closely

and a tingle of apprehension runs down your spine when you realize that the impression is identical to that made by your own boot.

If you possess the Sommerswerd, turn to **28**.
If you do not possess this Special Item, turn to **167**.

319

You recite the familiar words of the Brotherhood spell *Lightning Hand* and point your index finger at the head of your mortal enemy. You feel a surge of power and a crackle of blue flame explodes at the tip of your finger, but the sudden noise alerts Wolf's Bane to your presence.

A split second before your bolt of energy reaches its target, Wolf's Bane throws himself to the floor. The bolt burns the back of his thigh, wounding him badly, but not so badly as to prevent him from scrambling to his feet and effecting a hasty escape.

Turn to **207**.

320

The two reptilians have exhausted their supply of arrows and are frantically working at the chain in an effort to lower their iron pot to the floor of the vault. You can see that it will only be a matter of minutes before they accomplish their task.

Anxious to evade them, you examine the portal for a lever or some other means to make it rise. To the left of the tunnel arch you discover two squares of opaque crimson gemstone separated by a small slot. The squares are similar in size and design to those you encountered at the entrance to the temple of Avaros. These, too, comprise a locking mechanism that controls this portal. By tapping upon each square a correct number of times you will cause the lock to disengage and the portal to rise.

You place your fingers lightly upon the squares and feel the tell-tale vibrations that are the key to deciphering the secret code. After only seconds you are able to determine that the first code is equal to the number of islands south of the Kirlundin island of Hemd.

The second code is equal to the number of villages that lie on the highway between the cities of Toran and Anskaven.

In order to discover the exact numbers that will

open the portal, consult the map at the front of this book.

When you think you know the two-digit solution, turn to the entry that is the same number as your answer.

If you cannot decipher the codes, turn instead to **213**.

321

Aided by your Kai skills, you manage to avoid the falling debris until you reach the base of the skull-rock. Here you are struck by a deluge of earth that knocks you down and pins your legs to the floor: lose 8 ENDURANCE points.

Your body may be injured but your spirit refuses to give up. Frantically you dig yourself free with your bare hands and crawl the last few remaining yards to the skull's mist-filled jaw. Gritting your teeth against the pain of your injuries, you stagger to your feet and enter the opening barely moments before the entire temple ceiling caves in.

In addition to the ENDURANCE points loss, you also lose 1 Special Item and 1 Backpack Item of your choice.

To continue, turn to **174**.

322

You let your arrow fly but it fails to find its mark. It shatters uselessly against the creature's steel skull, leaving no time for a second shot. You only just have time to unsheathe a hand weapon to defend yourself as the great metallic beast comes leaping through the darkness.

Mech-wulf: COMBAT SKILL 50 ENDURANCE 45

This creature is immune to all psychic attacks.

If you win this combat, turn to **5**.

323

'Follow me, my lords!' shouts Foilan, as he spurs his black mare along a narrow, cobblestoned street that wends its way through Tyso's shabby northern quarter. At a junction close by the city's main stables, he turns into an avenue that leads to the West Arch of the Old Necropolis.

When the Arch is less than a hundred yards distant, Foilan brings his horse to a halt and you reign in your steed beside him. Several dozen guards and rangers have gathered at the Arch and they have erected a barricade which completely blocks the entrance to the burial ground beyond. The Reeve-lieutenant tells you to wait here with your men while he goes forward to inform the guards of the situation and to tell them that you and your companions are not Kai impostors.

Patiently you wait for Foilan to complete his task. Then, on seeing his signal, you move forward and join him at the Western Arch. He shouts an order and hurriedly the guards pull aside a wagon which blocks the entrance, enabling the five of you to dismount and proceed into the necropolis on foot.

Aided by the moonlight, you lead your party along a gravelled path towards the centre of the burial ground, to where a tunnel-like opening has been excavated in the side of a mossy mound. On arriving at this shadowy entrance you stop to examine the surrounding area, to check for any clues that may help you track your quarry. You find no fresh prints and you sense no lingering aura of an evil that could betray his presence. Confident that it is safe to proceed, you enter the mound and lead your comrades down a wide stone ramp to an oval-shaped chamber. A dozen stone coffins, each carved with the likeness of its occupant, are laid out in a circle like the spokes of a wheel. The chamber is cold and unwelcoming, but it does not harbour any trace of evil. You are sure that the impostor has not set foot here.

On the far side of the burial chamber, opposite the ramp, there is a stairwell which descends deep into the catacombs below the necropolis. You go down these stairs until you come to a landing where a passage crosses from north to south. Black Hawk suggests that the party split in two and explore both ways, but you are not in favour of this idea. Splitting the party would make it easier for the impostor if he chose to launch an ambush. You peer along both passages and draw on your Grand Mastery skills to determine the best route to follow, but with little success. Neither passage looks especially inviting.

If you decide to enter and explore the north passage, turn to **275**.

If you choose to investigate the south passage, turn to **107**.

324

You enter the building at ground level and follow

your adversary's tracks to a mouldering hall at the rear of this derelict dwelling. From the cover of a shadowy alcove you watch as Wolf's Bane meets and converses with two warriors. They are both helmeted and clad in suits of close-fitting grey armour. They have shiny steel spears slung over their shoulders which radiate a faint hum of electrical power. Their meeting is brief. Wolf's Bane issues terse commands and the two warriors leave to enact his orders. As you watch them go, you hazard a guess that their mission is to find and kill you.

Wolf's Bane leaves the hall by a broken rear door. You wait for a few minutes, to reduce the risk that he may detect how near you are, and then you follow his trail. The rear of the building opens onto a wasteland of shattered rubble which is bisected by a dead stream of salty, acidic water. You follow your opponent's trail across this bleak and forbidding landscape, past sharp spires of crimson and jet that erupt through the dereliction to scratch the cloudy sky. Rust-red water encircles their bases, lending them a wholly sinister aspect. To your eyes it seems as if this blighted city has been impaled upon these cruel, towering spikes.

Beyond the spires you see Wolf's Bane descending a flight of stone steps that disappear into the ground. Suddenly he stops and looks in your direction; it is as if he has sensed you are on his trail. Instinctively you dive to take cover behind a broken wall, but as you hit the ground it collapses, dumping you unceremoniously into a cellar that is flooded with black, briny water.

XVIII.   As you watch the warriors go, you guess that their
mission is to find, and kill you.

Coughing and spluttering, you bob to the surface and reach out to grab at a stone step. It is the lowest of a flight of slime-smeared steps that rise out of the water and ascend to a trapdoor in the ceiling. Suddenly you see two fiery red eyes emerging from the darkness and your stomach churns. They belong to the hungry, rubbery-skinned creature that dwells in this dismal cellar. It reaches out to grab you with its taloned hands, but you avoid its attack by wrenching at its wrist, sending it somersaulting over your head to splash into the water. Quickly you attempt to pull yourself onto the slippery steps before this creature recovers and tries to attack again.

Pick a number from the *Random Number Table*. If you possess Grand Pathsmanship and Grand Huntmastery, add 2 to the number you have picked.

If your total score is now 4 or less, turn to **145**. If it is 5 or more, turn to **52**.

325

As the last of these ghoulish creatures falls to your lightning-swift blows, you leap over its body and race up the stairs to the balcony above. You spare one last glance at the hall below and then, when you are sure that you have left behind no survivors who could raise an alarm, you hurry into the arch beyond.

Turn to **50**.

326

You soon discover that the creature's iron collar

and chain prevent it from reaching you so long as you keep close to the cavern wall. Mindful of this, you skirt around the writhing serpent and inch your way carefully towards the tunnel. However, you have progressed only a few yards when you feel the floor sloping away. The water is getting deeper.

If you possess Magi-magic, turn to **234**.

If you do not possess this Grand Master Discipline, turn to **25**.

327

Your target is beyond the effective range of your power word, yet there is still sufficient energy in your attack to knock him down. However, use of this Discipline at such long range puts an unnecessary strain on your vocal chords: lose 1 ENDURANCE point.

Wolf's Bane struggles to his feet and he curses you, his teeth showing white against the green of the jungle as he spits out a mouthful of damp soil. Then he turns and disappears into the undergrowth. Determined that you are not going to let him get away so easily, you dash out of the tunnel and give chase.

Turn to **90**.

328

Your killing blow splits the vile creature in two, severing the venom sac located below its tongue. The small amount of fluid remaining in the sac splashes on your weapon and immediately it gives off wisps of acrid, green-grey smoke.

Unless the weapon you are using is a Special Item,

the acid quickly corrodes it and renders it useless (delete this weapon from your Weapons List).

If, before leaving this hall, you wish to search the shelves for useful items, turn to **271**.

If you choose not to search the shelves, turn to **12**.

329

Drawing on your newly acquired magic, you focus on the distant vent and carefully recite the words of the Brotherhood spell *Teleport*. For a few seconds your vision swims in and out of focus as your strength is sapped of the power that this spell requires (lose 4 ENDURANCE points). Then your sight becomes crystal clear and you feel yourself floating upwards through the air towards the apex of this gigantic cavern.

You have risen close to a mile above the canyon when suddenly you attract the unwanted attention of a gigantic dragonfly. Anxious to evade a probable attack, you concentrate harder upon your destination and will yourself to accelerate.

Pick a number from the *Random Number Table*. If you possess Assimilance, add 1 to the number you have picked.

If your total is now *3* or less, turn to **340**.

If it is *4* or higher, turn to **84**.

330

As you leave the chamber, the portal slides shut and your Iron Disc emerges from the slot. You take the disc and slip it back into your pocket as you retrace your steps to the junction. On arriving there, you continue ahead and begin your exploration of this new passageway.

Turn to **137**.

331

Before you lies a smoke-filled hall that reeks of death and decay. Only the floor appears to be solid, and yet when you stare down at its glassy surface, you see that it is honeycombed with thousands of cells, each one occupied by a tortured soul writhing in perpetual torment. The walls of this evil chamber are wreathed with sulphurous smoke, lit intermittently by shafts of crimson lightning. The foul substances which pass for air seethe with the tension of ferocious, evil energies.

From the centre of the floor there arises a slender domed plinth. Moments later, a wide dais rises beside it, upon which you see a visage of the Dark God, one that he favours whilst occupying his unholy throne hall. Nothing could have prepared you for the sight that now meets your gaze – it is the foulest you have ever seen.

Naar's favoured form is a great globular body, like that of a bloated spider, borne by a score of stunted limbs which emerge chaotically from the underside of a sac-like abdomen. His face hangs like a parody of a wrinkled old sow's yet with an evil-smelling black hole where one could expect a snout. The upper surface of his body is covered with pouches of vile fluids that trail wisps of black smoke, and his maw is studded with hundreds of blue-stained fangs. But it is the eyes that shock you most. The Dark God has the eyes of a man.

XIX. Before you is Naar, the foulest thing you have ever
seen.

Naar shifts his bloated body from the dais and slither-shuffles towards the plinth. A misshapen limb extends to the plinth and its domed cover retracts to reveal a wondrous and mysterious artifact. A second shock stuns your senses when you recognize the nature of this artifact. It is one of the most legendary items in all the long history of Magnamund. It is the fabled Moonstone of the Shianti!

Turn to **112**.

332

The toughness of the plant wall and the confines of the stem make it difficult for you to wield your weapon effectively. It takes you nearly half an hour to hack your way out of this plant, during which time you lose 2 ENDURANCE points due to fatigue.

To continue, turn to **230**.

333

As you pull yourself from under the creature's body, your hand brushes against a collar of steel that is fixed tightly around its muscular neck. Attached to this collar is a thin disc of iron engraved with runic symbols. (If you wish to keep this Iron Disc, record it on your *Action Chart* as a Special Item.)

You are now anxious to leave this place in case the creature's death cry has alerted others of its kind. By way of an iron staircase, you leave this cellar and emerge through a trapdoor into a street adjacent to the hall.

Turn to **71**.

334

You have come to the edge of a deep canyon. The verdant walls of this massive gorge are carpeted with a rainbow of colour and the air is alive with the busy noise of huge, buzzing insects. Everything is fecund and fertile and dripping with humid jungle heat. High above the gorge you glimpse for the first time the source of the light which illuminates this strangely wonderful realm. The canyon is set within a cavern, the walls of which seem to engulf the sky. At its apex there is an oval-shaped vent through which a concentrated shower of amber rays pours down, like sunbeams through a stained glass portal. You watch in awe as flights of dragonflies, each as large as a Vassagonian Itikar, circle languidly above the canyon on gossamer wings. They shimmer like streaks of liquid silver as they ride the thermal currents. The sight is one of great beauty, yet one you cannot fully enjoy. The instinct which led you to the rim of this gorge now tells you that the source of the power you seek lies several miles away and above, beyond the vent that is the source of this cavern's light. Carefully you consider your predicament and determine that in order to escape, you must reach the vent – an exit that lies more than a thousand feet above the rim of the gorge.

> If you possess Kai-alchemy (and wish to use it) and have attained the rank of Kai Grand Crown, turn to **329**.
> If you possess Kai-alchemy (and wish to use it), but have yet to attain the rank of Kai Grand Crown, turn to **146**.

If you do not possess this Discipline, or if you choose not to use it, turn to **116**.

335

You emerge through the steel roof of the tower and catch a fleeting glimpse of the rainswept city far below. Suddenly there is a tremendous flash, closely followed by the concussive blast of a terrific explosion. This shockwave hits you from behind, leaving you feeling as if you have just been kicked in the back by an angry mule.

Fortunately your winged mount is able to ride this shockwave which helps propel it upwards at great speed into the base of the thick black storm clouds.

Turn to **310**.

336

The passage leads to a landing where a circular staircase gives access to levels above. As you climb the stairs, you are filled with a growing sense of uncertainty and dread as you ponder what may await you in this alien tower. Yet these feelings of impending doom are quickly banished when you reach the third level, for here you pick up the trail of your adversary. Your tracking skills determine that his trail is fresh and you pursue it eagerly.

You pass through a maze of empty passageways which leads eventually to a large, circular hall. Cautiously you approach the entrance and peer inside. Your tracking skills and your curiosity are handsomely rewarded when you see Wolf's Bane; he is standing alone and he is unaware that you have found him.

Turn to **100**.

337

'This way, my lords!' shouts Foilan, as he spurs his black mare along a mist-wreathed street that snakes through Tyso's shabby northern quarter. The street is deserted yet many citizens witness your passing. Their eyes glint in the moonlight as they peep through the smoky yellow panes of their windows, their curiosity and fears awakened by the clatter of your horses' hooves.

At length the street opens onto a wider avenue which gently descends towards a sprawling expanse of derelict ground surrounded by a tall, moss-covered perimeter wall. Several dozen guards and rangers have gathered at a distant archway in this wall and, by magnifying your vision, you can see that they have erected a barricade which completely blocks the entrance to the burial ground beyond.

The Reeve-lieutenant tells you to wait here with your men. Then he goes forward to inform the guards of the situation and to tell them that you and your companions are not Kai impostors. On seeing his signal, you move forward and join him at the archway. At his command, the guards hurriedly clear away some of the rubble which fills the entrance, enabling the five of you to dismount and proceed into the necropolis on foot.

In the moonlight, the burial ground has a certain ghostly beauty. There is an aura of sad serenity surrounding its mouldering tombs as, with the passing of centuries, they crumble to dust and disappear with their secret memories of another age. But all is not what it seems. Your sixth sense detects the lingering aura of an evil entity that has invaded this place. A glance at your fellow Kai tells you that they, too, can sense its presence.

You clasp the Platinum Amulet and feel a tingling vibration run through the palm of your hand. The sensation grows stronger as you move along a weed-choked path which leads to a shadowy tomb. With the passage of the years this tomb has settled lop-sidedly into the soft Tysoan earth, yet a flight of damp stone steps descends to where its door once was. As you draw nearer, you notice that all that now remains of the door is a mound of broken rubble.

If you possess Telegnosis, turn to **256**.
If you do not, turn to **318**.

338

When you strike your final blow, the limbs of the Meghanic come adrift from its torso and it disintegrates into a heap of buckled metal. You sift through this scrap and discover nothing of value, save for the warrior's sword.

You leap over the battered remains and continue along this winding tunnel until you reach an empty chamber. Here you can feel a warm breeze and you sense that it comes from a stairwell in the far wall. When you investigate, you rediscover Wolf's Bane's footprints clearly imbedded in dust on the stone steps. You cast your hands over them and detect that this is not a false trail; your enemy passed this way sometime within the last hour.

Slowly you ascend the stairs and arrive at the arched entrance to a large, vaulted stone chamber. Gathered around a fountain set into its north wall are a group of six grey-skinned humanoids. They are busy drinking a clear, oily fluid that pours from the fountain's spout into a semi-circular trough. All are barefoot and clad in rags, and they are each armed with a spear and a bow. The only exit from this chamber appears to be an archway set high in the north wall. There is a balcony in front of it that can only be reached by two flights of stairs which rise up on either side of the fountain.

Quietly you observe the creatures slaking their thirsts, and you try to formulate a way in which you can get past them and reach the balconied exit in the north wall.

> If you possess a Bow, and the Discipline of Magi-magic, and have attained the rank of Kai Grand Guardian, turn to **138**.
>
> If you possess Kai-alchemy and have attained the rank of Grand Crown (and wish to use it), turn to **26**.
>
> If you do not possess these skills, or a Bow, or if you have yet to attain the required levels of Kai mastery, turn to **121**.

339

From the cover of a leafy bush you observe the primitive settlement for several minutes. (During this vigil, unless you possess the Discipline of Grand Huntmastery, you must eat a Meal or lose 3 ENDURANCE points.) But as time ticks by you become increasingly restless. The hut into which your enemy ran is a small, single-roomed hovel, yet you can detect no movement within it. Prompted by a gnawing fear that you may have allowed Wolf's Bane to escape, you move closer to the settlement under cover of the thick jungle foliage.

Turn to **285**.

340

You increase the rate of your ascent, but your sudden acceleration serves only to make you a more attractive target in the eyes of the predatory dragonfly. With a loud and angry buzzing noise, the creature comes soaring down upon your back like a hawk upon a bolting hare.

Golasyx: COMBAT SKILL 49 ENDURANCE 45

This creature is attempting to stab you with the tip of its spear-like proboscis as it swoops past, therefore you need only fight this combat for one round.

If you inflict an equal or greater ENDURANCE loss upon the enemy in this single round of combat, turn to **163**.

If you sustain a greater ENDURANCE loss than your enemy, turn to **221**.

341

You draw your divine blade and a radiant halo of golden flame caresses its razor-sharp edge. You raise the sword above your head and then strike out at the leading point of the approaching fire-bolt. There is a tremendous splash of fiery sparks as you connect with the bolt and send it arcing away to explode harmlessly against the wall of the shaft.

The Sommerswerd absorbs some of the energy of the fire-bolt which it transfers to you through its hilt: restore 3 ENDURANCE points.

To continue, turn to **37**.

342

As you pass close to the creature's barbed torso, you sense that inwardly it is struggling desperately to overcome the effects of the spell you have placed upon it. Its body begins to twitch as its great crushing coils go into spasm. Sensing that it is about to break free, you cast the spell again to reinforce its effect.

Your second casting of the spell keeps the serpent from breaking loose and swiping you with its deadly tail, but the double use of Old Kingdom magic takes its toll on your physical stamina (lose 5 ENDURANCE points). With the serpent subdued, you are able to reach the safety of the exit and make your escape unscathed.

Turn to **115**.

343

Alyss draws upon her powers to create a cocoon of energy to protect both her vulnerable body and the legendary Moonstone. Kekataag assaults this glowing shield with maniacal ferocity, his great two-handed axe drawing fiery sparks with every mighty blow. You can sense from the hatred which blazes in his supernatural eyes that he and Alyss are old enemies.

Naar is now aware of your true identity. He also senses that you have made no effort to reach the

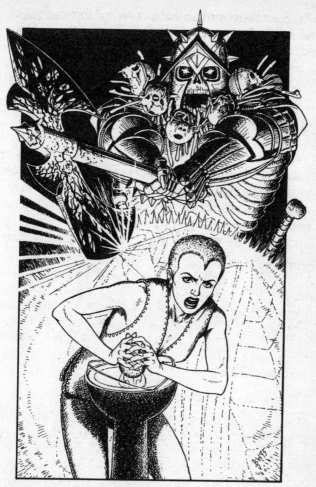

XX. Alyss creates a cocoon to protect herself and the
Moonstone.

Shadow Gate and so he moves away from Alyss, seemingly happy to allow his minion to press on with the attack while he devotes his undivided attention to you.

If you possess the Sommerswerd, turn to **132**.
If you do not possess this Special Item, turn to **147**.

You race along the passageway and turn the corner to see a tunnel sloping away into the gloom. The walls and ceiling are dripping wet, indicating to you that this dingy passageway passes directly under the stream. You hurry along its narrow confines, your shoulders grazing its muddy walls as you run, until you arrive at a flight of steps that ascend to an archway supported by thick wooden beams. Beyond the arch lies a large subterranean chamber that is daubed and decorated with runes and evil insignia. It is a primitive temple and it radiates an aura of evil so malicious that it makes your skin crawl.

On the far side of this unholy place, you see a stone altar standing before a huge boulder that has been crudely chiselled to resemble a grinning human skull. An eerie green glow pulsates from the eye sockets of this great skull-rock, and a mist swirls from its open jaw. Wolf's Bane is at the centre of the chamber but he is moving quickly towards the altar. You command him to stop and face you, but he ignores your order and continues running until he reaches the jaw of the great stone skull, which is flanked by two staves of iron set into holes in the ground. Gasping for breath, he now

turns to face you. For a moment his evil eyes dart
towards one of the iron staves and he reaches out
a hand as if to grasp it. But, seemingly, he changes
his mind. He sees you entering the temple and he
turns and runs into the open jaw of the skull to be
swallowed up by the roiling mist.

Quickly you pursue him, confident that you can
maintain the upper hand so long as you do not
lose his trail.

Turn to **140**.

345

Beyond where the illusory north wall once stood,
you can now see a small antechamber which is
wreathed in acrid blue smoke. Gradually this
smoke dissipates to reveal a shallow plinth upon
which lies a bronze urn. This heavy object rests on
its side and a quantity of pale grey ash has spilled
from its hinged lid. Cautiously you approach the
urn and see that there is an inscription engraved
on its side. From this ancient script you learn that
the ashes are the last remains of Baroness Garrulen, the wife of Hul – third Baron of Tyso. Glinting
half-buried in the ash, you notice a ring encrusted
with crimson gemstones (if you wish to keep this
Ruby Ring, record it on your *Action Chart* as a
Special Item).

You are righting the urn on its plinth when you hear
Steel Hand calling you. He has found something
among the rubble which litters the floor at the rear
of the antechamber.

Turn to **35**.

346

Your efforts are rewarded when the dragonfly responds to your healing powers. Consciousness and strength return to its battered body and the creature is able to pull out of its dive before it is too late. It swoops deep into the cavernous moat of the tower to gather speed for its slow ascent into the clouds. As you climb past the top of the tower you see that the dragonfly pens have been completely destroyed by the explosion. Fire rages through the uppermost levels of the tower, and it is spreading quickly to the other levels below.

Turn to **310**.

347

You stop to use your Magnakai Discipline of divination, to determine which passage you should follow. Unfortunately, you are still unable to detect your adversary's trail and you cannot determine any difference between the two passages.

If you decide to explore the left corridor, turn to **95**.

If you choose instead to explore the right corridor, turn to **137**.

348

Your final blow cleaves the head from the chained serpent and sends it spinning into the air. It collides with the ceiling and rebounds to splash loudly into the mire. For a moment it bobs on the surface, its lifeless eyes glazed and opaque, then it sinks slowly beneath the foam. Breathless from the fight, you sheathe your weapon and wade across the slimy ichor-stained waters towards the mouth of the

tunnel where you make a hasty escape from this
hostile cavern.

Turn to **115**.

349

The warrior skids to a halt and stares down in
disbelief at the legs of his slain comrade that protrude from beneath the fallen cylinders. You seize
the chance to attack and you move up behind
him and leap onto his undefended back. He fights
tenaciously to free himself, but his struggle ends
abruptly when you rip a steel cable from the canister that is strapped to his back. There is a dull
boom, and an eruption of blue-white flame shoots
from the top of the canister, burning open the
back of his helm. The force of this blast hurls him
forwards and leaves him sprawled across the cylinders that cover his slain comrade. For a few
seconds a spidery net of pulsating light enshrouds
the two lifeless warriors, then it crackles and disappears, leaving behind an acrid stench of
scorched metal and roasted meat.

Turn to **21**.

350

As the last of the creatures dies, you leap over its
heaped body and stumble through the Shadow
Gate into a whirling oblivion. The last image that
burns itself into your memory is that of Alyss slowly
succumbing to the relentless blows from Kekataag's
axe. The memory of her fearless bravery streng-
thens your spirit and resolve to forever serve the
forces of Good against the accursed hordes of darkness.

Congratulations Grand Master – you have won a great victory over the forces of Evil. You have defeated Naar's sinister plan to destroy you and conquer all of Magnamund. But, as you return through the Shadow Gate to the land of your birth, you know that the fight against Evil is not yet over. If you are to prevent the Dark God from launching his armies of night into Magnamund, you must return to the Plane of Darkness and retrieve the fabled Moonstone. Only by doing so will Magnamund be safe from the ravages of Naar's unholy hordes.

It will be a supremely perilous mission, perhaps the most dangerous you have ever undertaken. If you possess the true courage of a Kai Grand Master, the ultimate quest awaits you in the climax to the Grand Master series, entitled:

THE CURSE OF NAAR

RANDOM NUMBER TABLE

8	5	3	1	6	2	9	7	3	1
0	3	6	1	7	4	8	0	6	5
7	8	6	4	5	0	4	2	1	4
4	3	7	6	1	5	8	1	0	1
8	7	9	4	2	6	0	3	9	0
2	9	4	7	8	0	7	5	8	6
9	3	1	0	5	8	2	6	9	7
7	4	6	2	8	5	9	8	2	5
5	0	2	8	2	5	4	6	1	8
8	6	2	6	5	4	1	8	5	0

Other great reads ⟋ from **Red Fox**

Further Red Fox titles that you might enjoy reading are listed on the following pages. They are available in bookshops or they can be ordered directly from us.

If you would like to order books, please send this form and the money due to:

ARROW BOOKS, BOOKSERVICE BY POST, PO BOX 29, DOUGLAS, ISLE OF MAN, BRITISH ISLES. Please enclose a cheque or postal order made out to Arrow Books Ltd for the amount due, plus 75p per book for postage and packing to a maximum of £7.50, both for orders within the UK. For customers outside the UK, please allow £1.00 per book.

NAME_____

ADDRESS_____

_____

Please print clearly.

Whilst every effort is made to keep prices low, it is sometimes necessary to increase cover prices at short notice. If you are ordering books by post, to save delay it is advisable to phone to confirm the correct price. The number to ring is THE SALES DEPARTMENT 071 (if outside London) 973 9700.

Joe Dever

LONE WOLF ADVENTURES

For the keen adventure gamebook player.

If you would like to order books, please send your request and the money due to:
ARROW BOOKS, BOOKSERVICE BY POST, PO BOX 29, DOUGLAS, ISLE OF MAN, BRITISH ISLES. Please enclose a cheque or postal order made out to Arrow Books Ltd for the amount due including 30p per book for postage and packing both for orders within the UK and overseas orders.

Whilst every effort is made to keep prices low, it is sometimes necessary to increase cover prices at short notice. Arrow Books reserve the right to show new retail prices on covers which may differ from those previously advertised in the text or elsewhere.

Joe Dever and John Grant

LEGENDS OF LONE WOLF – Novels

If you would like to order books, please send your request and the money due to:
ARROW BOOKS, BOOKSERVICE BY POST, PO BOX 29, DOUGLAS, ISLE OF MAN, BRITISH ISLES. Please enclose a cheque or postal order made out to Arrow Books Ltd for the amount due including 30p per book for postage and packing both for orders within the UK and overseas orders.

Whilst every effort is made to keep prices low, it is sometimes necessary to increase cover prices at short notice. Arrow Books reserve the right to show new retail prices on covers which may differ from those previously advertised in the text or elsewhere.

Other great reads from **Red Fox**

Spinechilling stories to read at night

THE CONJUROR'S GAME Catherine Fisher

Alick has unwittingly set something unworldly afoot in Halcombe Great Wood.

ISBN 0 09 985960 2   £2.50

RAVENSGILL William Mayne

What is the dark secret that has held two families apart for so many years?

ISBN 0 09 975270 0   £2.99

EARTHFASTS William Mayne

The bizarre chain of events begins when David and Keith see someone march out of the ground . . .

ISBN 0 09 977600 6   £2.99

A LEGACY OF GHOSTS Colin Dann

Two boys go searching for old Mackie's hoard and find something else . . .

ISBN 0 09 986540 8   £2.99

TUNNEL TERROR

The Channel Tunnel is under threat and only Tom can save it . . .

ISBN 0 09 989030 5   £2.99

Other great reads ✒ *from* **Red Fox**

The Millennium books are novels for older readers from the very best science fiction and fantasy writers

---

A DARK TRAVELLING Roger Zelazny

An 'ordinary' 14-year-old, James Wiley has lost his father to a parallel world in the darkbands. With the help of his sister Becky, James, the exchange student and Uncle George, the werewolf, James goes in search of his parent.

ISBN 0 09 960970 3 £2.99

PROJECT PENDULUM Robert Silverberg

Identical twins Sean and Eric have been chosen for a daring experiment. One of them will travel into the distant past. The other into the distant future. And with each swing of the time pendulum they will be further apart . . .

ISBN 0 09 962460 5 £2.99

THE LEGACY OF LEHR Katherine Kurtz

The interstellar cruiser *Valkyrie* is forced to pick up four sinister, exotic cats, much to the captain's misgivings. His doubts appear justified when a spate of vicious murders appear on board.

ISBN 0 09 960960 6 £2.99

CHESS WITH A DRAGON David Gerrold

The Galactic InterChange was the greatest discovery in history . . . but now it had brought disaster. Unless Yake could negotiate a deal with the alien in front of him, mankind would be reduced to a race of slaves.

ISBN 0 09 960950 9 £2.99

COMBAT RULES SUMMARY

1. Add your COMBAT SKILL to any extra points given to you by your Kai Disciplines.

2. Subtract the COMBAT SKILL of your enemy from this total. This number = Combat Ratio.

3. Pick number from *Random Number Table*.

4. Turn to *Combat Results Tables*.

5. Find your Combat Ratio on the top of chart and cross reference to random number you have picked. (*E* indicates loss of ENDURANCE points to Enemy. LW indicates loss of ENDURANCE points to Lone Wolf.)

6. Continue the combat from Stage 3 until one character is dead. This is when ENDURANCE points of either character fall to 0.

TO EVADE COMBAT

1. You may only do this when the text of the adventure offers you the opportunity.

2. You undertake one round of combat in the usual way. All points lost by the enemy are ignored, only Lone Wolf loses the ENDURANCE points.

3. If the book offers the chance of taking evasive action in place of combat, it can be taken in the first round of combat or any subsequent round.

COMBAT RE

Combat Ratio

		−11 OR GREATER	−10/−9	−8/−7	−6/−5	−4/−3	−2/−1
Random Number	1	E −0	E −0	E −0	E −0	E −1	E −2
		LW K	LW K	LW −8	LW −6	LW −6	LW −5
	2	E −0	E −0	E −0	E −1	E −2	E −3
		LW K	LW −8	LW −7	LW −6	LW −5	LW −5
	3	E −0	E −0	E −1	E −2	E −3	E −4
		LW −8	LW −7	LW −6	LW −5	LW −5	LW −
	4	E −0	E −1	E −2	E −3	E −4	E −
		LW −8	LW −7	LW −6	LW −5	LW −4	LW −
	5	E −1	E −2	E −3	E −4	E −5	E −
		LW −7	LW −6	LW −5	LW −4	LW −4	LW −
	6	E −2	E −3	E −4	E −5	E −6	E −
		LW −6	LW −6	LW −5	LW −4	LW −3	LW −
	7	E −3	E −4	E −5	E −6	E −7	E −
		LW −5	LW −5	LW −4	LW −3	LW −2	LW −
	8	E −4	E −5	E −6	E −7	E −8	E −
		LW −4	LW −4	LW −3	LW −2	LW −1	LW −
	9	E −5	E −6	E −7	E −8	E −9	E −1
		LW −3	LW −3	LW −2	LW −0	LW −0	LW −
	0	E −6	E −7	E −8	E −9	E −10	E −1
		LW −0	LW −0	LW −0	LW −0	LW −0	LW −

E = ENEMY   LW = LONE WOL